Ultimate One Minute Explanations to GMAT® OG 13 Sentence Correction Questions

Copyright, Legal Notice and Disclaimer:

Aristotle Prep Ultimate One Minute Explanations to OG13 Sentence Correction Questions

10-digit International Standard Book Number: 9350872870

13-digit International Standard Book Number: 978-9350872871

Publisher: Aristotle Prep

Contents

Introduction

There is unanimous agreement among students and teachers alike that the Official Guide (OG) to the GMAT has the best collection of practice questions for the GMAT. Specifically with reference to the Sentence Correction section, there is a lot a student can learn by going through the official explanations given in the OG. However, one grouse that a lot of students have is that the OG explanations tend to be very lengthy and technical, at times almost impossible to understand for the average student. The students complain that there is no way they can arrive at the correct answer in less than a minute if they were to follow the methodology described in the OG.

Given this background, we decided to ask the subject matter experts at Aristotle Prep that if they were to attempt each of the questions in the OG 13 Sentence Correction section, how would they go about doing the same. What are the things that they would notice in each sentence and how would they eliminate options. The final objective was to arrive at the answer in less than a minute. This book is a compilation of their responses to this question. It is not an attempt to provide better explanations than the Official Guide but more practical and faster explanations. In a lot of the questions, we won't even be bothering with identifying all the errors. If we can get to the answer by identifying just one or two errors, that's good enough.

However, we haven't just limited ourselves to providing you these one-minute explanations from our experts. We realise that an average student, or even an above-average one, might not be able to spot errors as quickly and effectively as the experts at Aristotle Prep who have years of experience in the subject matter. In fact students regularly say that they are not able to identify the errors in a sentence or that they aren't sure of what to look for in a sentence.

So, in addition to providing you with one-minute explanations for each question, we decided to come up with an additional structured method of approaching Sentence Correction questions, a method that could be applied to every Sentence Correction question irrespective of the error type and difficulty level being tested. We've called this the Aristotle Multiple-Split Method.

The Aristotle Multiple-Split Method

As the name suggests, the Aristotle Multiple-Split Method of approaching Sentence Correction questions involves performing several splits one after the other in a fixed sequence.

Here is the order of the splits:

1) **Idiom Split** – In a lot of the questions, if you can identify the correct idiom you can immediately arrive at the correct answer or at least narrow down your choices to two options. So the first step is to always look for idioms in the underlined part of the sentence.

2) **First-word Split** - Try splitting and grouping the options on the basis of the fist word of every option. In case the first word is the same for all the options you can consider the first two or three words together.

3) **Last-word Split** – Similar to the first-word split but use the last word of every option instead of the first. Again in case the last word is the same for all the options you can consider the last two or three words together.

4) **Pronoun Split** – Split the options on the basis of pronouns in the underlined part.

5) **Verb Split** - Split the options on the basis of verbs in the underlined part.

6) When all else fails, check the remaining options for **Meaning**

In most of the questions you will be able to arrive at the answer well before you reach the verb-split stage, but in some tricky ones you might still have two or more options left after you have done this last split. In such cases the last step is to always check the remaining options for meaning. The option that conveys the meaning most clearly and using the least number of words will be the correct answer. At this stage you may have to make use of vague and subjective terms such as 'awkward wording' and 'not sounding correct' to eliminate options. This is fine because these will be high-difficulty questions and the difference between or among options will be very subtle.

It might appear that doing so many splits will take a lot of time but, in fact, it will only take around 10-15 seconds per split and in a lot of the questions you will arrive at the answer in two or three splits itself. The questions on which you require all the five splits and also the last step of checking for the meaning will most likely be high-difficulty ones so it makes sense to spend a little extra time on them anyway.

The beauty of the Aristotle Multiple-Split Method lies in the fact that it provides students with a structured method of approaching sentence correction questions, irrespective of the error type being tested or the difficulty level of the questions. Instead of reading a question and hoping that you will be able to spot the error, the Aristotle multiple-split method makes you actively look for specific errors and eliminate options on the basis of these. It makes a student feel more in control of the question, even in the case of difficult questions.

So to sum it all up, each question number in this book corresponds to that question in the Sentence Correction chapter in OG 13. For each question you will have two separate explanations – a One-minute explanation and an explanation using the Aristotle Multiple-Split Method. There will of course be some overlap between the two methods but the approach will be entirely different for the two.

We again reiterate that the OG has the best explanations and we strongly recommend that you go through them. Use this book as a supplement to know how a question can be attempted faster and without bothering too much with the technical nitty-gritty's of the question.

We hope you find this book useful in your prep. As always, we look forward to your feedback on how we could make this book better. Please mail us your feedback on feedback@aristotleprep.com

Good luck and practice hard!

Q1) The One-minute Method

While all the options begin with *psychologists,* the second word can actually give us a split – *declaring* vs. *declared.* We need the verb *declared* and not the participle *declaring* (in which case the sentence won't have a main verb at all)

a) A and B go out because of *declaring*

b) Eliminate D because we use *such as* and not *like* to give examples

c) Between C and E, we again require the verb form *have* or *had* and not the participle *having*. **Hence E is the correct answer.**

The Aristotle Multiple-Split Method

Idiom Split

A – such….as
~~B – such….like~~
C – such….as
~~D - such….like~~
E - such….as

To give examples we always use *such as;* hence eliminate B and D

First word Split

~~A – psychologists, declaring~~
C - psychologists declared
E - psychologists declared

We need the verb form *declared;* hence eliminate A

Last word Split

C – family size
E - family size

Doesn't help since both the options end with the same words

Pronoun Split

Doesn't help since both the options use *that* correctly

Verb Split

C – having failed
E – had failed

The verb is actually missing in C because *having* is a participle.

Hence E is the correct answer.

A - Verb
B – Verb, Idiom
C – Verb
D - Idiom
E - OA

Difficulty Level - Low

Q2) The One-minute Method

The first word and the last word split, on their own, may not give us an answer but looking at the two together we can easily spot a parallel construction between *the higher* and *the longer* i.e. *the higher X goes the longer Y will go.* Hence eliminate A, B, and E.

a) Between C and D, D unnecessarily adds the pronoun *it* and makes the sentence wordier. **Hence C is the correct answer.**

The Aristotle Multiple-Split Method

Idiom Split – No Idioms underlined

First word Split:

A – if
B – rating
C – the higher
D – the higher
E – when

Doesn't help much because none of the options can be conclusively eliminated

Last word Split:

A – longer
B – longer
C – longer
D – longer that
E – longer it is

Doesn't help much because none of the options can be conclusively eliminated

Pronoun Split:

~~A – they~~
~~B – it~~
C – None
~~D – it~~
~~E – it~~

It's always suggested that we avoid pronouns in the correct answer as much as we can. C has no pronoun and is also the shortest answer that correctly conveys the meaning.

Hence C is the correct answer.

A – Pronoun
B – Pronoun
C – OA
D – Pronoun
E - Pronoun

Difficulty Level – Low

Q3) The One-minute Method

The split, using the first word of the underlined part, gives us both, singular and plural verbs, and past and present tenses. Since the subject is singular *surge*, the verb also has to be singular. To get an idea of the correct verb tense always read the part of the sentence that is not underlined. The sentence states that 'some economists *say*'; *say* is in the present tense, so the first part of the sentence should also be in some form of the present tense.

a) A is out because of the plural *have*

b) In B, C & E, *raised* and *had raised* are in the past tense. Also we should try to avoid *being*.

c) *Has raised* is in the present perfect tense, hence **D is the correct answer**.

The Aristotle Multiple-Split Method

Idiom Split – No Idioms underlined

First word Split

~~A - have~~
~~B – raised~~
~~C – had~~
D - has
~~E - raised~~

Some options start with the past tense and some with the present tense. To figure out which tense we need to go with, read the part of the sentence that is not underlined. The line 'many economists *say*' tells us that we need a verb in the present tense since *say* is in the present tense. Hence eliminate B, C, and E.

But now what do we see – A has the plural *have* whereas D has the singular *has* - a classic case of subject-verb agreement. Since the subject is the singular *surge*, the verb also has to be singular, i.e. *has*

Hence D is the correct answer.

A – Subject verb agreement
B – Tense
C – Tense
D – OA
E – Tense

Difficulty Level - Low

Q4) The One-minute Method

The moment you see *not only* in the sentence, you should immediately check for the construction *not only....but also*. This eliminates A, D, and E.

a) Again whenever you come across a *not only.....but also* construction, always check the part after *not only* and after *but also* for parallel structure. In C, *arrange* is not parallel with *to mirror*. **Hence B is the correct answer.**

The Aristotle Multiple-Split Method

Idiom Split

~~A – not only....but as well~~
B – not only....but also
C – not only....but also
~~D – not only....but~~
~~E – not only....but as well~~

The correct idiom is *not only.....but also*; hence eliminate A, D, and E

First word Split

B – someone
C – someone

Doesn't help much because both the options begin with the same word

Last word Split

B – to finish
C – finishing

We always try to avoid *'-ing'* constructions. Also in C it appears that *in finishing* is referring to *style.*

Hence B is the correct answer.

A – Idiom
B - OA
C - Parallelism
D - Idiom
E – Idiom

Difficulty Level – Low

Q5) The One-Minute Method

A split using the first words does not prove to be of much help but a split using the last word proves useful – *as* vs. *than*. Remember, with *more/less* you always use a *than*.

a) Options A & B are out because of the use of *as* instead of *than* at the end

b) If you can't spot a difference amongst the remaining three options, look for verbs and pronouns. In this case two of the options (C & D) use the present tense *is* while one uses the past tense *was*. Since the sentence is speaking about a past event, the use of the present tense is incorrect. **Hence E is the correct answer.**

c) Alternatively, had you spotted the verb tense problem at the beginning itself, you could have simply checked the verbs in the five options and immediately arrived at the answer E without even bothering with the remaining parts of the other four options.

The Aristotle Multiple-Split Method

Idiom Split

~~A – more.....as~~

~~B - more......as~~

C - more.....than

D - more.....than

E – more......than

Eliminate A and B because the correct idiom is *more.....than*

First word Split

C - perhaps

D - maybe

E – perhaps

Doesn't help because *perhaps* and *maybe* can be used interchangeably.

Last word Split

C - than

D - than

E – than

Doesn't help because all the options are the same

Pronoun Split

C - it
D - it
E – no pronoun

C and D look needlessly long and also have the ambiguous pronoun *it* so ideally E should be the correct answer. If you are still unsure, do a verb split.

Verb Split

~~C – is~~
~~D – is~~
E – was

Since the sentence is talking about a past event, the verb needs to be in the past tense.

Hence E is the correct answer.

A – Idiom
B - Idiom
C - Tense
D - Tense
E – OA

Difficulty Level – Low

Notice that even though we needed several steps to arrive at the correct answer we have put this question in the 'Low difficulty' category. This is because we did not have to resort to vague and subjective considerations (such as awkward sounding options) to arrive at the correct answer. For all that you know you could have arrived at the correct answer immediately upon reading the question had you noticed the verb split.

Q6) The One-Minute Method

Doing a split using the first words gives us some singular *(ranks, has)* and some plural verbs *(rank, are, have)*. The subject is the singular *Diabetes* because of the usage of the additive phrase *together with.*

a) Singular subject *Diabetes* needs a singular verb. Hence options B, D, and E go out.

b) Between A & C, C is unnecessarily wordy. Also *only* is used as an adjective on the GMAT so it should come closer to the noun *heart disease* and not to the verb *surpassing*. **Hence A is the correct answer.**

The Aristotle Multiple-Split Method

Idiom Split

A – ranks as

B – rank as

~~C – rank of~~

D – no idiom

E – ranked as

The correct idiom is *rank as* so eliminate C.

First word Split

A - ranks

~~B - rank~~

~~D - are~~

~~E - have~~

Option A is singular whereas B, D, and E are plural. Since the subject is the singular *Diabetes,* the verb also needs to be singular. *(Do not be confused into thinking that the subject is plural because of the usage of the additive phrase 'together with'. For more on additives, go through the Subject-verb agreement section in the SC Grail)*

Hence A is the correct answer.

A – OA

B – Subject-verb agreement

C – Idiom

D – Subject-verb agreement

E – Subject-verb agreement

Difficulty Level – Low

Q7) The One-Minute Method

The first word split doesn't help much but the last word split eliminates B and C because we need the singular pronoun *it* to refer to the singular noun *eye*.

a) Among the remaining options do a split using the verb *–help/helps*. Since the subject is singular *structure,* the verb needs to be the singular *helps*. **Hence E is the correct answer.**

The Aristotle Multiple-Split Method

Idiom Split – No idioms underlined

First word Split

A – having
B – having
C – having
D – with
E - with

Doesn't help much because none of the options can be conclusively eliminated *(though 'having' is best avoided on the GMAT)*

Last word Split

A – it
~~B – they~~
~~C – they~~
D – it
E – it

The singular noun *eye* will agree with the singular pronoun *it*; hence eliminate B and C.

Pronoun Split - Already done above

Verb Split

A – help
D – help
E – helps

The singular subject *structure* will agree with the singular verb *helps*.

Hence E is the correct answer.

A – Subject verb agreement
B – Pronoun agreement
C – Pronoun agreement
D – Subject verb agreement
E – OA

Difficulty Level – Low

Q8) The One-Minute Method

Doing a split using the first words gives us two possibilities – *due to* and *because of*. We know that *due to* can only be used to replace *caused by* (which does not make sense in the context of this sentence), so we must go with *because of*.

a) A & B are out because of the use of *due to*

b) The usage of the phrase *within them* in C sounds ambiguous and you are tempted to remove this option, until you realize that all the three options make use of this phrase. So we need to look for something else.

c) You can approach the remaining three options in two ways from here:

   i. **Approach 1** – If you have understood the meaning of the sentence correctly, you might realize that the phrases *because tourists were exhaling moisture* and *because of moisture* don't logically follow from the earlier part of the sentence, whereas E does.

   ii. **Approach 2** – If the above reasoning looks too vague, do a split using the last words – *crystallize* and *crystallizing*. Don't blindly eliminate *crystallizing* because of the *-ing*. Read the part that is not underlined – it says *fungus was growing* so you need to go with *crystallizing* to parallel *growing*. **Hence E is the correct answer.**

The Aristotle Multiple-Split Method

Idiom Split – No Idiom

First word Split

~~A – due to~~
~~B – due to~~
C – because of
D – because of
E – because of

Since *due to* can only be used to replace *caused by* (which does not make sense in the context of this sentence), we must go with *because of.*

Last word split

~~C – crystallize~~
~~D – crystallize~~
E – crystallizing

Don't blindly eliminate *crystallizing* because of the *-ing*. Read the part that is not underlined – it says '*and* fungus was growing'. The usage of *and* suggests that there are two things that were happening and these two things obviously need to be parallel. So you need to go with *crystallizing* to parallel *growing*.

Hence E is the correct answer.

A – Usage
B – Usage
C – Parallelism
D – Parallelism
E – OA

Difficulty Level – Medium

Q9) The One-Minute Method

The first word split eliminates D and E because *percentage* by itself (i.e. when percentage is used as a subject) will always take *less* and not *fewer*. Among A, B, and C we need to check for comparison.

a) In A the subject is *production* so we cannot use the plural *those* to refer back to it.

b) In C we are comparing the *production* to the year *1978*, which is obviously wrong.

c) **B** correctly compares *production* with *harvest* and **is the correct answer.**

The Aristotle Multiple-Split Method

Idiom Split – No Idioms underlined

First word Split

A – less
B – less
C – less
~~D – fewer~~
~~E - fewer~~

Percentage by itself (i.e. when percentage is used as a subject) will always take *less* and not *fewer*. Hence eliminate D and E

Last word Split

A – harvest
B – harvest
C – 1978

Doesn't help much because none of the options can be conclusively eliminated

Pronoun Split

~~A – those~~
B – none
C - none

A incorrectly compares singular *production* with plural *those;* hence eliminate A

Verb Split

No verbs underlined. The main verb *reduced* is in the non-underlined part of the sentence.

Check the remaining options for Meaning

Most likely by this time you should have noticed the Comparison error (the use of *than* could be a clue). C incorrectly compares *production* to *1978*.

Hence B is the correct answer

A – Pronoun Agreement
B – OA
C - Comparison
D - Usage
E – Usage

Difficulty Level – Low

Q10) The One-Minute Method

The word *holds* needs to be followed by *that,* since the theory cannot possibly be holding *the beginning* or *the universe.*

a) D & E go out because they do not have *that*

b) Do a last-word split among the remaining three options. Since the original sentence implies that the universe is still expanding, the phrases *had been expanding* and *has expanded* are incorrect. **Hence A is the correct answer**.

The Aristotle Multiple-Split Method

Idiom Split – No Idioms underlined

First word Split

A - that
B - that
C - that
~~D – the (beginning)~~
~~E – the (universe)~~

In this sentence *holds* means the same thing as *claims* or *posits.* So it obviously needs to be followed by a *that.* D and E anyway don't make sense because the theory is not literally holding something.

Last word Split

A – has been expanding
~~B – had been expanding~~
~~C – has expanded~~

You can see that this is the same as doing a verb split. Since the expansion of the universe is still continuing, we need to go with the present perfect continuous tense – *has been expanding.*

Hence A is the correct answer.

A - OA
B – Tense
C - Tense
D - Usage
E - Usage

Difficulty Level – Medium

Q11) The One-Minute Method

Since the sentence starts with *Like* you immediately know that this is a Comparison question. Read the non-underlined part after the comma to figure out what actually needs to be compared. The non-underlined part contains the names of two people and you can only compare people with people.

a) Options A,B, C, and D are out because they compare *idolization* with *people*

b) Only E compares people with people, so **E is the correct answer**.

The Aristotle Multiple-Split Method

Idiom Split – No Idioms underlined

First word Split

~~A – Like~~
~~B – As~~
~~C – Like~~
~~D – As~~
E – Like

The usage of *Like* and *As* should immediately tell you that this is a comparison question. *Like* is used to compare nouns and *As* is used to compare everything other than nouns. To figure out what needs to be compared in this sentence, we need to read the part (that is not underlined) after the comma. It says *James Joyce and Virginia Woolf*. Since these are names of people, whatever is being compared also has to be people only. So we are comparing nouns; hence *As* goes out.

We don't need to do another split here. Since we have already identified that this is a comparison question, quickly check the remaining options to see which ones get the comparison right. If there is more than one such option then we'll do another split.

A and C compare *idolization* with *people;* E is the only option that compares *people* (Brontes and Brownings) with *people* (James Joyce and Virginia Woolf).

Hence E is the correct answer.

A - Comparison
B – Comparison
C - Comparison
D - Comparison
E – OA

Difficulty Level – Low

Q12) The One-Minute Method

Do a split using the first words. On the GMAT, *which* needs to be preceded by a comma, else its use is incorrect.

a) Options A & C are out because of the incorrect usage of *which*

b) The sentence is in the present tense and discusses a current situation, so the use of the past tense *kept* is incorrect. This eliminates E.

c) Though both B & D use some form of the present tense, we require the simple present tense *keeps* to parallel the rest of the sentence. **Hence the correct answer is B**.

The Aristotle Multiple-Split Method

Idiom Split – No Idioms underlined

First word Split

~~A - which~~
B - that
~~C - which~~
D - that
E – having

On the GMAT *which* always needs to be preceded either by a comma or by a preposition, else its usage is wrong. (Refer to the SC Grail *That vs. Which* for details). Hence A and C are out.

Last word Split

B - keeps
~~D - keeping~~
~~E - kept~~

Since a current situation is being discussed, the use of the past tense is incorrect. Hence E is out.

D unnecessarily uses the present perfect continuous tense *has been keeping*. We are discussing a situation that is a fact but isn't necessarily an ongoing action; hence the simple present tense *keeps* should be ideal.

Hence B is the correct answer.

A – Usage/pronoun
B - OA
C – Usage/pronoun
D - Tense
E - Tense

Difficulty Level – Low

Q 13) <u>The One-Minute Method</u>

A split doesn't prove to be of much help in this sentence. A hint for you is the use of the word *method* in the first part of the sentence because this invariably means that a method will be described to you and you'll need to put its various steps in the correct parallel form. The same is the case with this sentence. The underlined part is describing two steps in a method, so the first step should parallel the second. The moment you realize this, this sentence becomes very easy.

a) A is out because *the forming* is not parallel with *they are laid*

b) B is out because *forming* is not parallel with *to lay them*

c) C is out because *having* is not parallel with *they were laid*

d) E is out because *which* incorrectly refers to mud or clay

e) *To form* is parallel to *to lay*. **Hence D is the correct answer.**

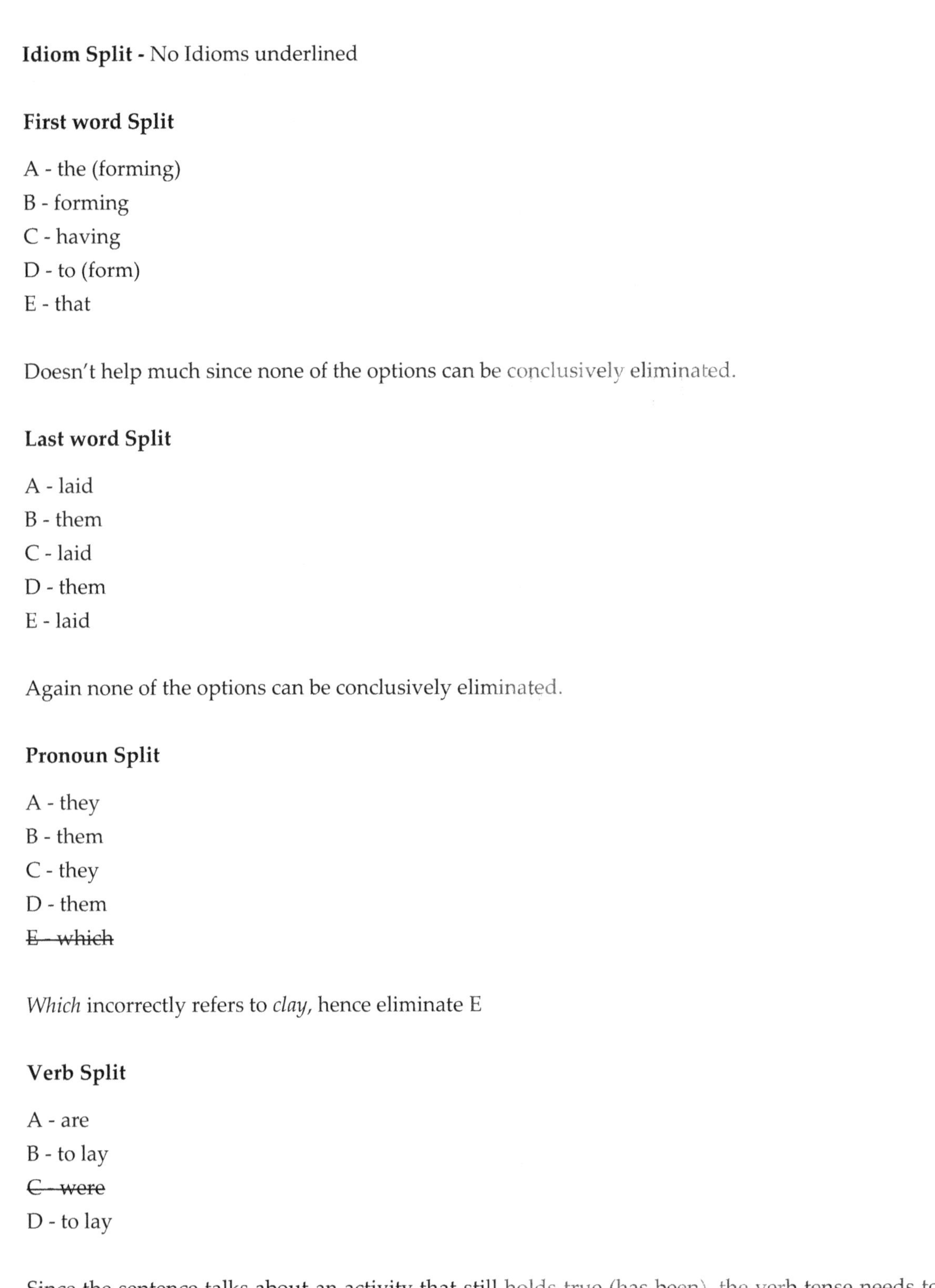

The Aristotle Multiple-Split Method

Idiom Split - No Idioms underlined

First word Split

A - the (forming)
B - forming
C - having
D - to (form)
E - that

Doesn't help much since none of the options can be conclusively eliminated.

Last word Split

A - laid
B - them
C - laid
D - them
E - laid

Again none of the options can be conclusively eliminated.

Pronoun Split

A - they
B - them
C - they
D - them
~~E - which~~

Which incorrectly refers to *clay,* hence eliminate E

Verb Split

A - are
B - to lay
~~C - were~~
D - to lay

Since the sentence talks about an activity that still holds true (has been), the verb tense needs to be present and not past. Hence eliminate C.

Check the remaining options for Meaning

A hint for you is the use of the word *method* in the first part of the sentence because this invariably means that a method will be described to you and you'll need to put its various steps in the correct parallel form. The same is the case with this sentence.

The underlined part is describing two steps in a *method* so the first step should parallel the second. A goes out because *the forming* is not parallel to *they are laid*. B goes out because *forming* is not parallel to *to lay them*. D correctly makes *to form* parallel with *to lay*.

Hence D is the correct answer.

A - Parallelism
B - Parallelism
C - Tense
D - OA
E - Usage

Difficulty Level - Medium

Q14) The One-Minute Method

You can do a first word split – *when* and *if*. On the GMAT, *when* is almost always used to refer to a time period. You can also do a last word split – *lead* and *leads* – and look for a subject verb agreement problem.

a) Options A, B, and C are out because of *when*. B also gets the subject verb agreement wrong with *leads*.

b) Between D & E, D is out because the singular verb *leads* does not agree with the plural subject *inventories*. **Hence E is the correct answer.**

The Aristotle Multiple-Split Method

Idiom Split - No Idioms underlined

First Word Split

~~A - when~~
~~B - when~~
~~C - when~~
D - if
E - if

On the GMAT *when* is used to refer to a specific time period whereas *if* is used to make a conditional statement. Obviously *if* will be preferred in this sentence.

Last Word Split

~~D - leads~~
E - lead

Since the subject is the plural *inventories*, the verb needs to be the plural *lead*.

Hence D is the correct answer

A - Usage
B - Usage
C - Usage
D - Subject-verb agreement
E - OA

Difficulty Level – Low

Q15) The One-Minute Method

The idiom being tested here is *not X but Y*. Hence eliminate A and B because they don't use a *but*.

a) Again whenever you come across a *not X but Y* construction, check for parallel structure after *not* and *but*. Since *not* is followed by *as*, *but* also needs to be followed by *as*. **Hence D is the correct answer.**

The Aristotle Multiple-Split Method

Idiom Split

~~A – not….rather~~

~~B – not…yet~~

C – not…but

D – not…but

E - not…but

The correct idiom is *not X but Y*, so eliminate A and B

First word Split

C – but a

D – but as

E – but also

The rule of parallel structure dictates that since *not* is followed by *as*, *but* should also be followed by *as*.

Hence D is the correct answer

A - Idiom

B - Idiom

C - Parallelism

D - OA

E - Parallelism

Difficulty Level – Low

Q16) The One-Minute Method

You need to be very careful while doing a split in this question for two reasons. The first is that the verb is not *claims* but *suggest(s)*, so essentially you are doing a second-word split. The second reason is that the moment students see the word *surge,* they assume that the verb will also be singular but the sentence actually talks about two things – *the surge and a drop.* Hence the verb needs to be the plural *suggest.*

a) D & E are out because the use of *suggesting* makes no sense.

b) B is out because of the use of the singular *suggests*

c) Between A & C, the use of *have* in C is incorrect. **Hence the correct answer is A.**

The Aristotle Multiple-Split Method

Idiom Split

A - as.....as (as weak as)
~~B - so.....as (so weak as)~~
C - as.....as (as weak as)
~~D - so.....as (so weak as)~~
E - as.....as (as weak as)

Since the correct idiom is *as.....as,* eliminate B and D

First Word Split

A – claims
C – claims
E – claims

Doesn't help since all the options are the same

Last Word Split

A - thought
C - analysts
E - analysts

Doesn't help because both the alternatives could be correct

Pronoun Split

A - that
C - that
~~E - no pronoun~~

On the GMAT, a verb such as *suggest* will almost always be followed by *that,* so eliminate E.

Verb Split

A - suggest, thought
~~C - suggest, have been thought~~

Eliminate C because the plural verb *have* cannot take the singular *economy* as a subject

Hence A is the correct answer

A - OA
B - Idiom
C - Verb Tense
D - Idiom
E - Usage

Difficulty Level - Medium

Q17) The One-Minute Method

A split doesn't prove too helpful so we need to go through each of the options and eliminate.

a) A looks good so you hold it.

b) B reverses the meaning of the sentence, so goes out

c) C looks ok so you hold it as well

d) D goes out because of the unnecessary use of *-ing* in *having*

e) E goes out because *which* incorrectly refers to the *sun's surface* and not to sun spots

f) Between A & C, A is better because C does not make clear what is never sighted. **So A is the correct answer.**

The Aristotle Multiple-Split Method

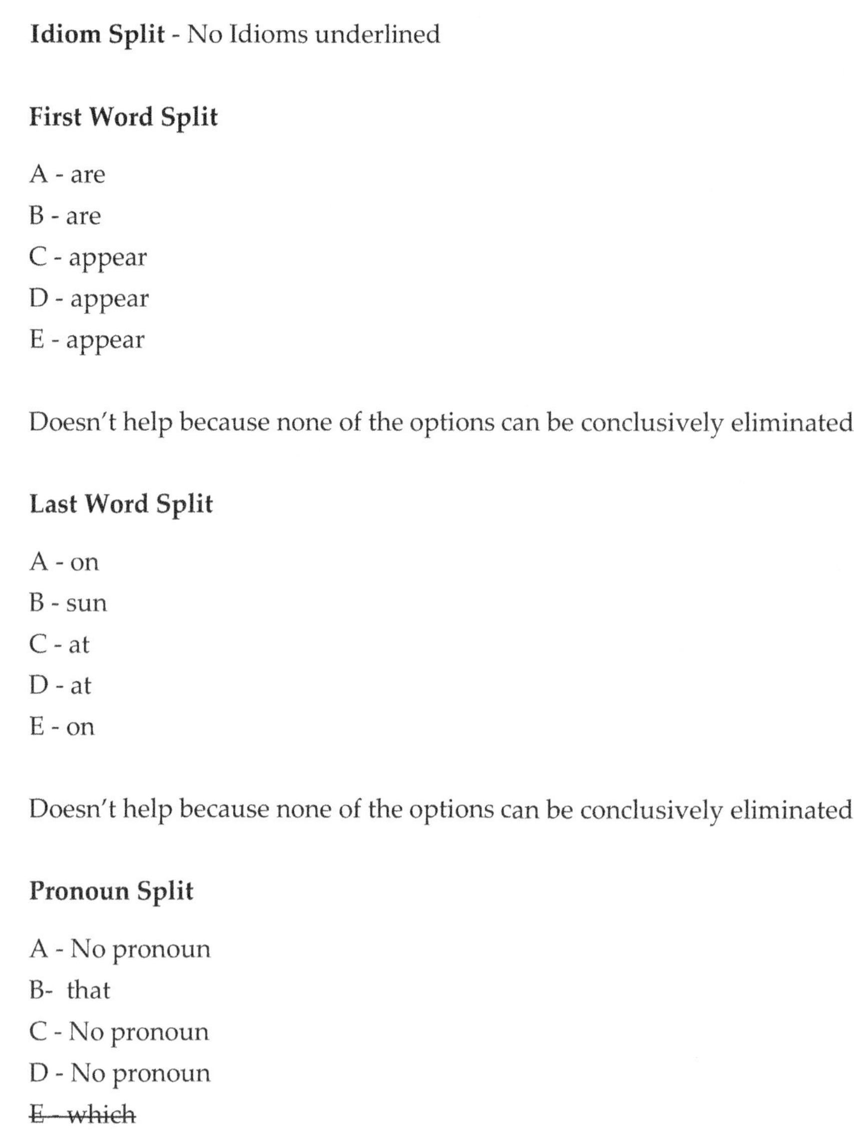

Idiom Split - No Idioms underlined

First Word Split

A - are

B - are

C - appear

D - appear

E - appear

Doesn't help because none of the options can be conclusively eliminated

Last Word Split

A - on

B - sun

C - at

D - at

E - on

Doesn't help because none of the options can be conclusively eliminated

Pronoun Split

A - No pronoun

B- that

C - No pronoun

D - No pronoun

~~E - which~~

Which incorrectly refers to the *sun's surface,* hence eliminate E.

Verb Split

A - are, have been sighted

B - are, have been sighted

~~C - appear, sighted~~

~~D - appear, having been sighted~~

Since the first part of all the options is in the present tense, the second part also needs to be in some form of the present tense. Hence eliminate C because it has the simple past tense *sighted.* Also eliminate D because *having been sighted* unnecessarily uses the continuous tense.

Check the remaining options for Meaning

Between A and B, B reverses the meaning of the sentence by suggesting that sunspots have never been sighted on the surface of the sun whereas the original sentence states exactly the opposite.

Hence A is the correct answer.

A - OA
B - Meaning
C - Tense
D - Tense
E – Usage

Difficulty Level - Medium

Q18) The One-Minute Method

You should ideally have spotted a list of items towards the end of this sentence and realized that it's a parallel structure question. The first two items in the list start with *revamp* and *institute,* so there is no way that the third item can start with an *-ing* word.

a) A, B, and C go out because of the use of *creating*

b) In D, you again avoid the *-ing* in *for taking,* **So the correct answer is E.**

The Aristotle Multiple-Split Method

Idiom Split- No Idiom

First Word Split

~~A - creating~~
~~B - creating~~

~~C - creating~~
D - and
E - and

To figure out which of the two alternatives is better we need to read the part of the sentence before the underline, and what do we see here - a list of things starting with *to* (to revamp, to institute). Since this is the last item in this list, we need to start with *and*. Hence A, B, and C are out.

Last Word Split

D - taking
E - take

The phrase *for taking* is considered unidiomatic on the GMAT. We anyways try to avoid *-ing* words at all times.

Hence E is the correct answer

A - Parallelism
B - Parallelism
C - Parallelism
D - Parallelism
E - OA

Difficulty Level – Low

Q19) <u>The One-Minute Method</u>

It is difficult to split up the options. Also since the options are not very long, it's best to read each option and eliminate.

a) A should be eliminated because the phrase *a pioneer journalist* is modifying Nellie Bly's exploits and not Nellie Bly.

b) B looks good so hold it.

c) C should be eliminated because, by changing *included* to *including*, the main verb has been eliminated from the sentence.

d) D should be eliminated because it uses the present tense verb *are* to refer to a past event.

e) E makes it appear as if the *pioneer journalist* and *Nellie Bly* were two different people.

f) **Hence B is the correct answer.**

The Aristotle Multiple-Split Method

First word Split

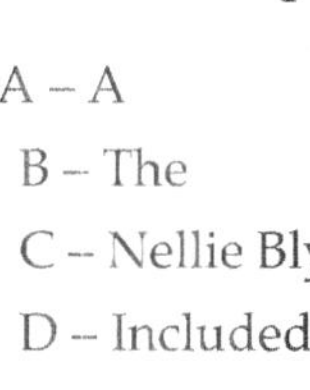

A – A
B – The
C – Nellie Bly
D – Included
E – The

Doesn't help much because none of the options can be conclusively eliminated

Last word Split

A – included
B – included
C – the
D – are
E – included

Doesn't help much because none of the options can be conclusively eliminated

Pronoun Split

A – none
B – none
C – her
D – none
E – none

C correctly uses *her* to refer to *Nellie Bly*. Hence none of the options can be conclusively eliminated

Verb Split

A – included
B – included
~~C – was~~
~~D – are~~
E – included

C does not contain the main verb *included*. D uses the present tense verb *are* to refer to an event in the past. Hence eliminate C and D.

Checking the remaining options for Meaning

A should be eliminated because the phrase 'a pioneer journalist' is modifying *Nellie Bly's exploits* and not *Nellie Bly*.

E makes it appear as if *the pioneer journalist* and *Nellie Bly* were two different people.

Hence B is the correct answer.

A - Modification
B - OA
C - Verb
D - Tense
E - Verb tense

Difficulty Level – Medium

Q20) The One-Minute Method

On the GMAT, words such as *expectations* will almost always be followed by *that*. Also, since the sentence is talking about a future event in the past (*'rose'*), *would* needs to be used.

a) C, D, and E are out because they omit *that*

b) Between A & B, the use of past tense *doubled* in A is incorrect because we are talking about something happening in the future. **Hence B is the correct answer**.

The Aristotle Multiple-Split Method

Idiom Split - No Idioms underlined

First Word Split

A - that
B - that
~~C - of~~
~~D - of~~
~~E - of~~

On the GMAT, words such as *expectations* will almost always be followed by *that*. Hence eliminate C, D, and E

Last Word Split

A - that of
B - double

Reading the part immediately after the underline gives you the answer. The phrase *that of the 1.4 percent growth rate* in A makes no sense because *that* has no antecedent.

Hence B is the correct answer

A - Meaning
B - OA
C - Usage
D - Usage
E – Usage

Difficulty Level - Medium

Q21) The One-Minute Method

The first-word split gives you a choice between *and* and *or*. The correct word should be *or* because all of these ingredients do not have to be present in a food for it to be not called *natural*. Even if one of these ingredients is present the food cannot be called *natural*.

a) C & E are out because of the use of *and*

b) A is out because the use of 'not contain' and 'nothing' together creates a double negative.

c) B is out because it distorts the meaning of the sentence – *that* actually refers back to food. **Hence D is the correct answer.**

The Aristotle Multiple-Split Method

Idiom Split - No Idioms underlined

First Word Split

A - or

B - or

~~C - and~~

D - or

~~E - and~~

Since a *natural* food should not contain any prohibited ingredient, the correct connector has to be 'or'. Hence eliminate C and E.

Last Word Split

A - has been

B - has been

D - has been

Obviously doesn't help. Notice that this is also a verb split (since all the alternatives are verbs)

Pronoun Split

Doesn't help much because the usage of *that* is correct in all the options.

Verb Split - Already done above

Check the remaining options for Meaning

A is out because the use of *not contain* and *nothing* together creates a double negative. B is out because it distorts the meaning of the sentence – 'that' actually refers back to food.

Hence D is the correct answer.

A - Meaning
B - Meaning
C - Meaning
D - OA
E - Meaning

Difficulty Level - Medium

Q 22) The One-Minute Method

The phrase immediately after the underline *in the form of carbon dioxide* must refer to what comes immediately before it. This has to be *carbon*. So you do a last-word split and eliminate all the options that do not contain *carbon* at the end.

a) A, B, and E go out because they do not contain *carbon* at the end

b) D is missing a verb, so **C is the correct answer.**

The Aristotle Multiple-Split Method

Idiom Split

A - more.....than
B - more.....than
C - more.....than
D - more.....than
E - more.....than

All the options get the idiom correct.

First Word Split

A - Plants
B - Plants
C - Plants
D - Plants
E - Plants

Doesn't help because all the options are the same

Last Word Split

~~A - fungi~~
~~B - fungi~~
C - carbon
D - carbon
~~E - fungi~~

Read the part immediately after the underline. This is a modifying phrase *in the form of carbon dioxide*. Now between carbon and fungi, what could this phrase possibly be modifying? Obviously *carbon*, so put this phrase next to carbon i.e. eliminate A, B, and E.

Pronoun Split - No pronouns underlined

Verb Split

C - are
D - no verb

Eliminate D since it does not have a verb anywhere in the underlined or non-underlined part.

Hence C is the correct answer.

A - Modification
B - Modification
C - OA
D - No Verb
E - Modification

Difficulty Level - Medium

Q 23) The One-Minute Method

A first-word split gives you a choice between two types of connectors – *and* which is used to continue a thought and *but* and *although* which are used to show contrast. The sentence is obviously trying to show the contrast between 'planters' and the activities of 'fishing and hunting'.

a) B & C are out because *and* does not show contrast

b) Avoid A & C because of the *'-ing'* form in *supplementing*. Also, if you read these two options back into the sentence, they don't make too much sense. **Hence the correct answer is D.**

The Aristotle Multiple-Split Method

Idiom Split - No Idiom

First Word Split

A - but
~~B - and~~
~~C - and~~
D - although
E - but

'But' and 'although' are connectors used to show contrast whereas 'and' is used to continue with the earlier thought. Now this sentence first tells us that the Iroquois were primarily planters. Then 'fishing' and 'hunting' don't logically flow from this fact, so the usage of 'and' would be incorrect. We actually need to show contrast in this sentence by using 'but' or 'although'.

Last Word Split

A - supplementing
D - supplemented
E - supplementing

Go with the simple past tense 'supplemented' to parallel the simple past tense 'were' earlier in the sentence.

Hence D is the correct answer.

A - Verb tense

B - Meaning

C - Meaning

D - OA

E - Verb tense

Difficulty Level - High

Q24) The One-Minute Method

The usage of the words *'as contrasted'* in the underlined part immediately tells you that this is a Comparison question. The part after the comma has the insect *'yellow jacket'* so the part before the comma must also have an insect.

a) B, C, and D are out because they compare *something* of the honeybee or the sting of the honeybee with the yellow jacket

b) Between A & E, 'unlike' sounds better than 'as contrasted with' (which is an incorrect idiom), **so E is the correct answer**.

The Aristotle Multiple-Split Method

Idiom Split – No idioms underlined

First-word split

A – As contrasted

B – In contrast

C – Unlike

D – Unlike

E – Unlike

The break-up of the first words should immediately tell you to look for a comparison error. To figure out what is being compared, look at the part of the sentence that is not underlined (most likely after a comma). It says *'the yellow' jacket'*, which is an insect, so the part before the comma should also mention an insect only.

Now let's see what each of the options is comparing with the yellow jacket.

A - honeybee
~~B - honeybee's something~~
~~C - sting~~
~~D - something of the honeybee~~
E - honeybee

A and E are the only options that compare the honeybee with the yellow jacket, so eliminate B, C, and D.

Between A and E, A is longer and unidiomatic.

Hence E is the correct answer.

A - Unidiomatic
B - Comparison
C - Comparison
D - Comparison
E - OA

Difficulty Level - Low

Q25) <u>The One-Minute Method</u>

This question looks difficult at first but becomes easy if you do a last-word split. Some options have the verb '*are*' and some do not. You obviously can't have a sentence without a main verb so the options that do not contain '*are*' go out.

a) D & E go out because they do not contain a verb at the end. Even though D has a verb 'have' in the middle, the part after the underline doesn't make sense with the rest of the sentence

b) Among A, B, and C, again do a last-word split. Do we require an 'and' before the 'are'? Obviously not, **hence A is the correct answer.**

The Aristotle Multiple-Split Method

Idiom Split - No Idioms underlined

First word Split

A - Neuroscientists
B - Neuroscientists
C - Neuroscientists
D - Neuroscientists
E - Neuroscientists

Doesn't help because all the options are the same.

Last word Split

A - are
~~B - and are~~
~~C - and are~~
D - , (comma)
E - , (comma)

On reading the sentence carefully we notice that the part between the commas is simply modifying 'Neuroscientists'. We obviously need a verb 'are' to go with Neuroscientists. However the usage of 'and' before 'are' makes no sense because the sentence does not talk about two things. Hence eliminate B and C.

Pronoun Split

A - its
D - its
E - its

Doesn't help because 'its' correctly refers to 'brain' in all the options

Verb Split

A - are
~~D - have amassed, now drawing~~
~~E - have amassed, now drawing~~

The phrase 'now drawing' doesn't make sense by itself. It should at least be preceded by 'are' to imply that 'Scientists have amassed and scientists ***are*** now drawing'.

Hence A is the correct answer.

A - OA
B - Meaning
C - Meaning
D - Meaning
E - Meaning

Difficulty Level - High

Q26) The One-Minute Method

Since the sentence contains a list of items (the important roles played by the bat), we need to check for parallel construction. Since *'aiding'* is the first item in the list and it is not underlined, the remaining items also must use the *'-ing'* construction. **B** is the only option that gets this right and **is the correct answer**.

The Aristotle Multiple-Split Method

Idiom Split - No Idiom

First word Split

A – pollinating
B – pollinating
C – pollinating
~~D – they~~
~~E – they~~

Since we have a list of items start with an '-ing' word 'aiding', we need to go with *pollinating*. Hence eliminate D and E.

Last word Split

A – produce
B – produce
C – produce

Doesn't help because all the options are the same

Pronoun Split

A – None

B – None

~~C – they~~

The use of *they* in C breaks the parallel structure; hence eliminate C

Verb Split - No verbs are underlined

Check the remaining options for Meaning

You would have definitely spotted the parallel construction by now. Since all the items in the list need to have the *'-ing'* construction, A can be eliminated

Hence B is the correct answer

A - Parallelism

B - OA

C - Pronoun

D - Parallelism

E - Parallelism

Difficulty Level – Medium

Q27) The One-Minute Method

A simple parallel structure question. The phrase *'do not commit crimes'* can only be parallel with another phrase that contains the word *'do'* to imply *'do commit crimes'*. **D is the correct answer** since only D contains 'do'.

The Aristotle Multiple-Split Method

Idiom Split - No Idioms underlined

First word Split

~~A - have~~
~~B - has~~
~~C - shall~~
D - do
~~E - could~~

The first part of the sentence says why some people *do not* commit crimes so the second part has to parallel that by saying why some people *do* commit crimes.

Hence D is the correct answer.

A - Parallelism
B - Parallelism
C - Parallelism
D - OA
E - Parallelism

Difficulty Level - Medium

Q28) The One-Minute Method

Do a first word split and avoid the *'-ing'* in trying' Anyways 'organism's attempt' sounds better than 'organism's trying'.

a) A and B are out because of the use of 'trying'

b) C & D go out because the phrase *'attempt to try'* is redundant since *to attempt* is the same as *to try*. **Hence the correct answer is E.**

The Aristotle Multiple-Split Method

Idiom Split - No Idioms underlined

First word Split

~~A - trying~~
~~B - trying~~
C - attempt
D - attempt
E - attempt

'Organism's' cannot be followed by 'trying', the correct phrasing has to be an organism's 'attempt'. So A and B go out.

Last word Split

C - irritant
D - it
E - irritant

Doesn't help much because none of the options can be conclusively eliminated.

Verb Split

C - attempt
D - attempt
E - attempt

Doesn't help because all the options are the same.

Check for Meaning

You should immediately be able to spot the redundancy. 'Attempt' and 'try' mean the same thing so to use them together in a sentence is redundant.

Hence E is the correct answer

A - Awkward
B - Awkward
C - Redundancy
D - Redundancy
E - OA

Difficulty Level - Medium

Q29) The One-Minute Method

This is another question that looks difficult at first but becomes simple if you do a last-word split – *outnumber* and *outnumbering*. We always try to avoid the *'-ing'* constructions; also the use of outnumbering at the end of the sentence doesn't make sense because we are trying to say that 'letters' outnumber other 'letters'.

a. A, C, and D are out because of the usage of 'outnumbering'

b. Between B and E, the use of 'begins' to denote a past time period is incorrect. **Hence E is the correct answer**.

The Aristotle Multiple-Split Method

Idiom Split - No Idiom

First word Split

A – Dickinson were
B – Dickinson were

C - Dickinson,

D - Dickinson,

E - Dickinson,

Cannot really eliminate anything based on this

Last word Split

~~A - outnumbering~~

B - outnumber

~~C - outnumbering~~

~~D - outnumbering~~

E - outnumber

Now look at the sentence as a whole and try to figure out the meaning that it is trying to convey - A's letters to B *outnumber* A's letters to anyone else. It will obviously be incorrect to use 'outnumbering' in this sentence, so eliminate A, C, and D.

Pronoun Split

B - No pronoun

E - Which

You could be tempted to eliminate E because the pronoun 'which' is not referring to Susan Huntington Dickinson but before this just go through B once and check for the verb.

Verb Split

B - begins, ended

E - outnumber

Since 'begins' and 'ended' are not parallel in terms of the tense, we eliminate B.

Hence E is the correct answer

A - Usage

B - Tense

C - Usage

D - Usage

E - OA

Difficulty Level – High

Q30) The One-Minute Method

If you know your idioms, this question can be done in ten seconds. The correct idiom is estimated 'to be', **hence D is the correct answer.**

The Aristotle Multiple-Split Method

Idiom Split

~~A - estimated at~~
~~B - estimated as~~
~~C - estimated that~~
D - to be
~~E - as~~

When used with reference to a time period, the correct idiom is *'estimated to be'*.

Hence D is the correct answer.

A - Idiom
B - Idiom
C - Idiom
D - OA
E - Idiom

Difficulty level - Low

Q31) The One-Minute Method

The use of 'unlike' at the beginning of the sentence immediately tells you that this is a Comparison question. The part after the comma starts with Barbara McClintock so the part before the comma also must have a person as subject. But the tricky part is that, apart from the first option, no other option uses 'unlike'; all the other options actually change the first sentence into a modifying phrase that modifies Barbara McClintock.

a) A goes out because it compares 'conviction' with Barbara McClintock

b) Avoid B, C, & E because of the usage of 'being'. If the remaining option does not look good, then come back and check these out.

c) D actually looks very good, so don't go back to the earlier options. **D is the correct answer**.

The Aristotle Multiple-Split Method

Idiom Split - No Idioms underlined

First word Split

~~A - Unlike~~
B - Although
C - Contrary
D - Even (though)
E - Even with

Whenever you see 'unlike' you need to check for comparison. Option A incorrectly compares 'conviction' with 'Barbara McClintock' so should be eliminated

Last word Split

~~B - being~~
C - were
D - were
~~E - being~~

'Being' is almost always incorrect on the GMAT so keep out options B and E for now. In case you can't find the answer from between C and D then go back and check B and E, else don't waste your time and move on.

Pronoun Split

B - her
C - her

Both the pronouns correctly refer to Barbara McClintock

Verb Split

C - being
D - were

As discussed earlier, avoid 'being' and go with the simple past tense 'were'.

Hence D is the correct answer

A - Comparison
B - Usage
C - Usage
D - OA
E - Usage

Difficulty level - Medium

Q32) <u>The One-Minute Method</u>

You should be able to spot the idiom immediately – *the same to someone…..as to someone.*

a) A is out because it does not contain '*to*'

b) D and E are out because 'the' refers to a specific person and hence distorts the meaning of the sentence

c) Between B & C, C is longer and also the semi colon is not required in C, hence **B is the correct answer**.

The Aristotle Multiple-Split Method

Idiom Split

~~A - same to someone.......as~~
B - same to someone.......as to
~~C - No idiom (Usage of semi colon breaks the idiom)~~
~~D - same to someone.......as it would to~~
~~E - No idiom (Usage of semi colon breaks the idiom)~~

The correct idiom is '*same to X.....as to Y*'.

Hence the correct answer is B

A - Idiom
B - OA
C - Idiom
D - Idiom
E - Idiom

Difficulty level - Medium

Q33) The One-Minute Method

Do a first word split – *because* and *due to*. 'Due to' can only be used to replace 'caused by', so doesn't make sense in this sentence.

a) D and E are out because of the use of 'due to'

b) B is out because 'which' incorrectly refers to 'computer chips'

c) Between A and C, C should be eliminated because it is unnecessarily wordy and also uses the ambiguous pronoun 'which'; **hence A is the correct answer**.

The Aristotle Multiple-Split Method

Idiom Split - No Idiom

First word Split

A - Because
B - Because
C - Because
~~D - Due to~~
~~E - Due to~~

'Due to' can only be used to replace 'caused by', it cannot be used to replace 'because of'; hence eliminate D and E.

Last word Split

A - plunging
B - oversupply
C - oversupply

Doesn't help since none of the options can be conclusively eliminated

Pronoun Split

A - No pronoun
~~B - which~~
~~C - which~~

The usage of 'which' in both B and C is ambiguous since 'which' should ideally refer to what comes immediately before the comma.

Hence A is the correct answer

A - OA
B - Pronoun
C - Pronoun
D - Usage
E - Usage

Difficulty level - Low

Q34) The One-Minute Method

A first-word split gives you the choice between *if* and *whether*. 'If' is used to make a conditional statement whereas 'whether' is used to evaluate alternatives. Hence the usage of 'if' is incorrect in this sentence.

a) A is out because of the usage of 'if'

b) D and E are out because the phrases 'for broadening' and 'the ability for it' are unidiomatic.

c) Between B and C, C can be eliminated because it is unnecessarily wordy and also distorts the parallel structure. **Hence B is the correct answer**.

The Aristotle Multiple-Split Method

Idiom Split

~~A - depends on if~~
B - depends on whether
C - depends on whether
~~D - depends on its~~
~~E - depends on the~~

Whenever a sentence talks about the happening of two things (broaden and leave) the correct idiom will be 'depends on whether', so eliminate A, D, and E.

First word Split

B - whether (it can)
C - whether (or not)

Both the options have the same first word so look at the next word. Ideally the usage of 'or not' with whether is not required since this is already implied in the use of *whether*. So B should be the correct answer but if you are still unsure go to the next step.

Last word Split

B - and leave
C - and can leave

Again, since the last words are the same, look at one or two words before that. The usage of 'and' tells you to look for parallel construction. In C 'to broaden' must be matched with 'to leave' or simply 'leave'. It cannot be parallel to 'can leave'.

Hence B is the correct answer

A - Idiom
B - OA
C - Parallelism
D - Idiom
E - Idiom

Difficulty level - Low

Q35) The One-Minute Method

a) The use of *and* in A makes no sense. Also A and B use the idiom '*so…that*' incorrectly. Hence eliminate A and B

b) The use of 'so' and 'such' in D is redundant, hence eliminate this as well.

c) Between C and E, 'where' cannot be used to refer to time; hence eliminate C. **E is the correct answer.**

The Aristotle Multiple-Split Method

Idiom Split

~~A - so…for~~
~~B - so…..for~~
C – so….that
~~D - so…..such that~~
E – so….that

The correct idiom is *so that* or *such that*; hence eliminate A, B, and D

First word Split

C – earning
E – earned

Ideally the answer should be E because we always try to avoid *'-ing'* constructions, but let's continue anyway.

Last word Split

C – were
E – were

Doesn't help because both the options are same

Pronoun Split

C – these, where, she
E – when, she

In C, the use of *where* to modify time is incorrect. *Where* is always used to refer to a place.

Hence E is the correct answer.

A - Idiom
B - Idiom
C – Pronoun/Usage
D – Idiom/Redundancy
E -OA

Difficulty level - Low

Q36) The One-Minute Method

Another easy question if you know your idioms. The correct idiom is '*seem to*'; **hence C is the correct answer**.

The Aristotle Multiple-Split Method

Idiom Split

~~A - seem like it is indicative~~

~~B - seem as if to indicate~~

C - seem to indicate

~~D - seem indicative~~

~~E - seem like an indication~~

With 'indicate' the correct idiom is always 'seem to indicate'.

Hence C is the correct answer.

A - Idiom

B - Idiom

C - OA

D - Idiom

E -Idiom

Difficulty level - Low

Q37) The One-Minute Method

This sentence mentions three things about Deborah Sampson – joined, was injured and was discharged. These three things need to be in parallel structure, but the important thing to note is that the first of these '*joined*' was done by Deborah Sampson herself whereas the other two (*injured and discharged*) were done to her by someone else. Hence these two items need to be preceded by 'was' to show that someone else has done these to Deborah Sampson.

a) B is out because 'while' breaks the rule of parallel structure

b) C is out because of the usage of 'being'; also it doesn't use 'was' before discharged

c) D is out because it omits the 'was' before injured

d) Avoid the '-ing' in *having* and also avoid *being*. Hence **A is the correct answer**.

The Aristotle Multiple-Split Method

Idiom Split - No Idioms underlined

First word Split

A - was
~~B - was~~
~~C - and was~~
~~D - injured~~
~~E - having been injured~~

Since the first word - 22 - is the same for all the options look at the next few words to do a split. The sentence says three things about Deborah Simpson - she joined, she was injured, and she was discharged. Only A gets this order right.

Note: You could also keep out B, C, and E because of 'being'

Hence A is the correct answer.

A - OA
B - Parallelism
C - Parallelism
D - Parallelism
E – Parallelism

Difficulty level – High

Q38) The One-Minute Method

The correct idiom is *admiration for*; hence eliminate D and E.

a) Again in any sentence the part before and after the 'and' needs to be parallel. So in A *'the person'* needs to parallel *'the politician'* and not *'as a politician'*. Hence eliminate A.

b) Similarly in C, since *not only* is followed by 'as', *but also* needs to be followed by *'as'* as well. **Hence B is the correct answer.**

The Aristotle Multiple-Split Method

Idiom Split

A – admiration for
B – admiration for
C – admiration for
~~D – admiration of~~
~~E – admiration of~~

The correct idiom is admiration for; hence eliminate D and E

First word Split - Already done above

Last word Split

~~A – had been~~
B – was also
C – was also

We need the simple past tense *'was'* to parallel the simple past tense *'had the greatest admiration'* earlier in the sentence. Hence eliminate A, because it uses the past perfect tense.

Pronoun Split - No pronouns underlined

Verb Split

B – was
C – was

Both the options use the verb correctly

Check the remaining options for Meaning

The use of *'not only'* in C means we should check this option for parallel construction. Since *'not only'* is followed by 'as', *'but also'* needs to be followed by 'as' as well.

Hence B is the correct answer

A - Tense
B - OA
C - Parallelism
D - Idiom
E - Idiom

Difficulty level - Medium

Q39) The One-Minute Method

Whenever you spot the word 'so' in a sentence, look for one of these two idioms – *'so…that'* or *'so…..as to'*. This immediately gives you **the correct answer as A**.

a) B and D are missing a *'that'*

b) The phrase *'is it'* in C makes it appear as if a question is being asked.

c) The usage of *'economical'* in E distorts the meaning of the sentence

The Aristotle Multiple-Split Method

Idiom Split

A - so....that
B - no idiom
C - so....as to
D - no idiom
E - so....that

All the idioms have been used correctly so none of the options can be eliminated at this stage.

First word Split

A - it

B - it

C - so

D - such

~~E - there~~

The word 'there' should almost always be avoided on the GMAT, so you can keep out E for now.

Last word Split

A - economic

~~B - economical~~

C - economic

~~D - economical~~

'Economical' does not mean the same thing as 'economic', so eliminate B and D.

Pronoun Split

A - it

C - it

Both the pronouns correctly refer to 'Schistosomiasis'

Verb Split

A - is, has become

C - is, become

The verb usage is correct in both the sentences

Check the remaining options for meaning

The GMAT prefers the idiom '*so....that*' to '*so.....as to*'. Also between A and C, A sounds more complete whereas C sounds awkward.

Hence A is the correct answer

A - OA

B - Meaning

C - Meaning

D - Meaning

E – Meaning

Difficulty level - Low

Q40) The One-Minute Method

Doing a first word split gives us a choice between *only* and *but only*.

a) In the overall context of the sentence the use of 'but' is not required as the conditional connotation is already implied by the use of 'only'. Hence eliminate A and B.

b) Eliminate D because the use of 'were trimming' does not make sense as the sentence is not talking about a continuous action in the past.

c) Between C and E, C is in the passive voice; **hence E the correct answer.**

The Aristotle Multiple-Split Method

Idiom Split - No idioms underlined

First word Split

~~A – year, but only~~
~~B – year, but only~~
C – year only
D – year only
E – year only

In the overall context of the sentence the use of '*but*' is not required as the conditional connotation is already implied by the use of '*only*'. Hence eliminate A and B.

Last word Split

C – would be trimmed
D – were trimming output
E – trim output

The verb in C is passive and the use of the past continuous tense in D is also not required.

Hence E is the correct answer.

A - Redundancy
B - Redundancy
C - Passive verb
D – Verb Tense
E – OA

Difficulty level – Medium

Q41) The One-Minute Method

Doing a first-word split gives us two options – *arguing* and *a treatise*. The part before the comma mentions the name of a book – *Discourse on Women* – so the part after the comma should ideally be a description of this book, hence it cannot start with a verb 'arguing'.

a) A and B are out because of the usage of 'arguing'

b) If you are confused among the remaining options look at the part that is after the underline – it starts with *'and for changes....'*. The usage of 'and' tells you that whatever comes before 'and' has to be parallel with what is coming after 'and'. Hence we require a *'for'* in the underlined part of the sentence, **so the answer is E**.

The Aristotle Multiple-Split Method

Idiom Split - No Idiom

First word Split

~~A - arguing~~
~~B - arguing~~
C - a treatise
D - a treatise
E - a treatise

Since the first word comes after a comma it is most likely a modifying phrase modifying *'Discourse on women'*. The correct word therefore should be 'a treatise' because it describes 'Discourse on women'. The sentence is not saying that the 'Discourse on women' is doing (*arguing*) something.

Last word Split

C - rights
D - rights
E - women

Doesn't help since none of the options can be conclusively eliminated.

Pronoun Split

C - that
D - no pronoun

E - that

Doesn't help since none of the options can be conclusively eliminated.

Verb Split

C - advocates
D - advocating
E - argued

While 'advocating' unnecessarily uses the '*ing*' construction, it may not be reason enough to eliminate this option. Let's check the options for meaning.

Check the remaining options for meaning

When you are confused in a sentence, it always helps to read the part that is not underlined. The usage of the phrase 'and for changes' tells you that something has to come before 'and' and this thing should match what is coming after 'and' i.e. it also has to start with the preposition 'for'.

Hence E is the correct answer

A - Modification
B - Modification
C - Parallelism
D - Parallelism
E - OA

Difficulty level - Medium

Q42) The One-Minute Method

Doing a first word split give you two options – *have* and *would have.* Since the sentence is talking about a hypothetical situation, you obviously need to go with *'would have'* You can also do a last-word split and eliminate all the options that give you *'economical'* because this distorts the meaning of the original sentence.

a) A and B go out because of *'have'*

b) C goes out because of *'economical'*

c) Between D and E, E gets the comparison wrong by comparing *'what demographers need to know'* with *'now'*. Hence **the correct answer is D.**

The Aristotle Multiple-Split Method

Idiom Split

A - more...than
B - more...than
C - more...than
D - more...than
E - more...than

While all the options use *'more....than'* correctly, you should realise that this phrase is used to show comparison. So check whether all the options get the comparison right.

~~A - compares 'would have to know' with 'now'~~
B - compares 'would have to know' with 'they do now'
C - compares 'would have to know' with 'they do now'
D - compares 'would have to know' with 'they do now'
~~E - compares 'would have to know' with 'now'~~

A and E obviously go out because they compare logically incomparable things - *knowledge* and *now.*

First word Split

~~B - have~~
C - would
D – would

We need to go with the conditional *'would'* since the sentence is talking about a hypothetical situation. So eliminate B.

Last word Split

C - economical
D - economic

The usage of *'economical'* is incorrect since it distorts the meaning of the sentence.

Hence D is the correct answer

A - Comparison
B - Verb
C - Usage
D - OA
E - Comparison

Difficulty level – Medium

Q43) The One-Minute Method

While a split doesn't help much, the first line of the sentence should tell you that you are looking at a comparison question. The *land area of Laos* needs to be compared with the *land area of Great Britain*, and all the options that don't do this go out.

a) A and B go out because they get the comparison incorrect

b) C goes out because *'them'* has no antecedent.

c) Between D and E, the use of 'and' in D distorts the meaning of the sentence, so **E is the correct answer**.

The Aristotle Multiple-Split Method

Idiom Split - No Idiom

First word Split

~~A - about~~
~~B - of~~
C - that
D - comparable
E - comparable

The usage of '*comparable*' in two of the options should tell you that this is a comparison question. A and B incorrectly compare Laos' land area with Great Britain (and not with Great Britain's land area), so eliminate them.

Last word Split

~~C - them~~
D - many
E - whom

The usage of '*them*' in C is unclear; it's better to use the relative pronoun '*whom*'. So eliminate C.

Pronoun Split

D - No pronoun
E - whom

It's better to go with the relative pronoun '*whom*' to refer to 'people'. Also the usage of 'and' in D does not make sense because we are not talking about two different/separate things.

Hence E is the correct answer.

A - Comparison
B - Comparison
C - Pronoun
D - Meaning
E – OA

Difficulty level - Medium

Q 44) The One-Minute Method

The moment you see a *'between'*, look for an *'and'* to eliminate the options that get this idiom wrong.

a) A and D are out because *'between….with'* is an incorrect idiom.

b) B can be eliminated because it makes no sense

c) Between C and E, E can be eliminated because it is not as clear as C is in explaining who the rivalry is between. Hence **C is the correct answer**.

The Aristotle Multiple-Split Method

Idiom Split

~~A - between……with~~
B - No Idiom
C - between….and
~~D - between….with~~
E - No Idiom

The correct idiom is *'between….and'*, so eliminate A and D. The answer will most likely be C, but you still need to check the other two options that don't use an idiom.

First word Split

~~B - rivals~~
C - rivalry
E - active

The plot can centre on rivals A and B, it cannot centre on the rival A against B. So eliminate B. Now you should feel even more confident that C will be the correct answer. Quickly go through E to check whether you can find some problem with this. The phrase *'and the rivalry'* does not make clear whose rivalry we are talking about.

Hence C is the correct answer
A - Idiom
B - Meaning
C - OA
D - Idiom
E – Meaning

Difficulty level – Medium

Q45) The One-Minute Method

The moment you spot the word *'believe'* in the sentence, check for the correct idiom i.e. *'believe to be'*.

a) D and E are out because they get the idiom wrong

b) Among A, B, and C, if you do a first-word split you will notice that B starts with a verb while the other two options do not. Immediately go back and check whether the sentence contains a verb in the first place. It does not, so you need to add the verb. Hence **B is the correct answer**.

The Aristotle Multiple-Split Method

Idiom Split

A - believed to be

B - believe to be

C - believe to be

~~D - believe are~~

~~E - believed are~~

The correct idiom is *'believe to be'*, so eliminate D and E.

First word Split

~~A - believed~~

B - are

~~C - some~~

Since two of the options (A and B) supposedly give you verbs, check the sentence for other verbs to get an idea of the tense and agreement that is required. What do you notice? A and C have no verbs. In A you might be tempted to think that 'believed' is a verb but 'believed to be' is just a participial phrase. It needs a helping verb such as 'are' before it. Similarly C also lacks this verb.

Hence the correct answer is B

A - Verb

B - OA

C - Verb

D - Idiom

E – Idiom

Difficulty level – Low

Q 46) The One-Minute Method

Doing a split doesn't help much in this sentence, but on reading the whole sentence you should realize that it is giving you two things on which ancient Thai artisans expended their energy – *creation of Buddha images* and the *construction and decoration of temples*. These two things need to be in parallel structure.

a) A, C, and D are out because they get the parallel structure wrong.

b) Between B and E, E goes out because it is unnecessarily wordy and also has the pronoun 'they' at the end. Hence **B should be the correct answer**.

The Aristotle Multiple-Split Method

Idiom Split

~~A - expended for~~
B - expended on
C - expended on
D - No idiom
E - No idiom

The correct idiom is '*expended on*', so eliminate A.

First word Split

B - much
C - much
D - creating
E - the (creation)

Doesn't help because none of the options can be conclusively eliminated.

Last word Split

B - enshrined
C - enshrined
D - them
E - them

Doesn't help much because none of the options can be conclusively eliminated. 'Them' correctly refers back to the plural noun 'images'.

Pronoun Split - Already done above

Verb Split

B - was expended
C - was expended
D - accounted
E - accounted

Doesn't help because all the options use the verb correctly.

Check the remaining options for meaning

The usage of 'and' and 'as well as' should immediately tell you that two things are mentioned in the sentence so look for parallel construction in each of the options.

B - on the creation.......on the construction
~~C - on the creation.....constructing and decoration of~~
D - No clear parallelism
~~E - the creation of......construction and decoration of~~

C and E get the parallelism wrong so eliminate them. (E needs a 'the' before 'construction and decoration of')

Between B and D, D sounds very awkward because of the usage of 'and'. Also B uses the correct idiom.

Hence B is the correct answer

A - Idiom
B - OA
C - Parallelism
D - Awkward
E - Parallelism

Difficulty level - High

Q47) The One-Minute Method

If you know your idioms then a last-word split can come in really handy on this question. Remember that *'pronounced'* the way it is used in this sentence (to mean *'declared'*) does not take anything with it – no *'as'* or *'with'* or anything else.

a) C and D are out because they use *'as'* with pronounce

b) E goes out because the use of *'it'* at the end of the sentence is redundant/ambiguous

c) Between A and B, 'taking' in A makes no sense so **B is the correct answer.** It also makes *'took'* and *'pronounced'* parallel.

The Aristotle Multiple-Split Method

Idiom Split

A - pronounced
B - pronounced
~~C - pronounced as~~
~~D - pronounced as~~
~~E - pronounced it~~

When you are talking of *'pronounced'* to mean *'stated'* or *'claimed'* then pronounced will not take anything. 'Pronounced as' is used to refer to the actual pronunciation of a word. Hence eliminate C, D, and E.

First word Split

A - his translation of
B - his translation of

Doesn't help because both the options are the same.

Last word Split

A - pronounced
B - pronounced

Doesn't help because both the options are the same.

Pronoun Split

A - his, him
B - his, him

Doesn't help because both the options use the pronouns correctly

Verb Split

A - no verb
B - took

You might think that '*taking*' in A is a verb but the fact that it comes after a comma means it is being used a participle. A in fact does not have a main verb at all.

Hence B is the correct answer

A - Verb
B - OA
C - Idiom
D - Idiom
E - Idiom

Difficulty level - High

Q48) The One-Minute Method

Apply the rule for '*which*' and eliminate A and B because in these '*which*' incorrectly refers to the earth.

a) Eliminate D because the use of *though* and *but* together is not required as they both show contrast. The use of '*it*' too doesn't make sense.

b) Between C and E, in E what follows the opening phrase should be the *Caspian Sea* and not the *largest lake* on earth; **hence C is the correct answer.**

The Aristotle Multiple-Split Method

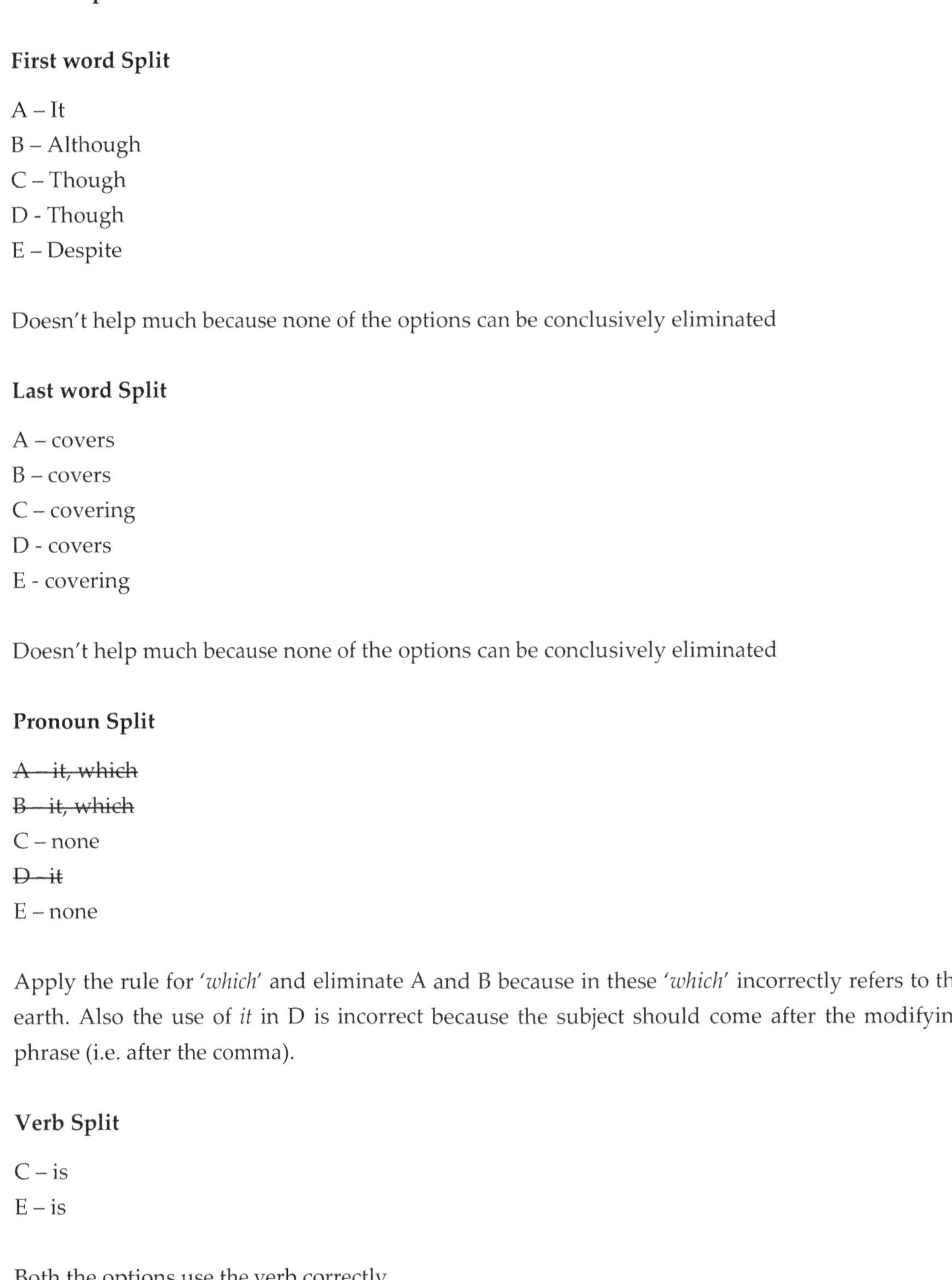

Idiom Split - No idioms underlined

First word Split

A – It
B – Although
C – Though
D - Though
E – Despite

Doesn't help much because none of the options can be conclusively eliminated

Last word Split

A – covers
B – covers
C – covering
D - covers
E - covering

Doesn't help much because none of the options can be conclusively eliminated

Pronoun Split

~~A – it, which~~
~~B – it, which~~
C – none
~~D – it~~
E – none

Apply the rule for *'which'* and eliminate A and B because in these *'which'* incorrectly refers to the earth. Also the use of *it* in D is incorrect because the subject should come after the modifying phrase (i.e. after the comma).

Verb Split

C – is
E – is

Both the options use the verb correctly

Check the remaining options for Meaning

Between C and E, in E what follows the opening phrase should be the Caspian Sea and not the largest lake on earth.

Hence C is the correct answer

A - Pronoun
B - Pronoun
C - OA
D - Pronoun
E - Modification

Difficulty level - Medium

Q49) The One-Minute Method

What follows *'reduced'* should be *'time'*, so do a first-word split and eliminate all the options that don't start with *'time'*.

a) A and E are out because they do not start with 'time'

b) B and C are out because of the usage of 'being'. Hence **D is the correct answer**.

c) Remember *'being'* is not always incorrect on the GMAT, so had option D not looked good to us, we would have gone back and checked options B and C. But since D looks very good, we don't need to waste time. We can move to the next question.

The Aristotle Multiple-Split Method

Idiom Split - No Idiom

First word Split

~~A - from~~
B - the (time)
C - the (time)

D - the (time)

~~E - from~~

Since the word immediately before the underline is *'reduced'*, what follows should be whatever is being reduced i.e. the *time*. Hence eliminate A and E.

Last word Split

B - minutes

C - minutes

D - minutes

Doesn't help because all the options are the same.

Pronoun Split - No pronouns underlined

Verb Split

~~B - being required~~

~~C - being required~~

D - required

B and C unnecessarily use 'being'.

Hence D is the correct answer

A - Meaning

B - Verb Usage

C - Verb Usage

D - OA

E - Meaning

Difficulty level - Medium

Q50) The One-Minute Method

We start with a first-word split. Now you can't be confident *'in something'*. You can be confident '*that* something will happen' or you can have confidence 'in someone's ability'.

a) B and D are out because they use the phrase *'confidence in the economy'*.

b) C goes out because the middle line of C doesn't sound good.

c) Between A and E, E goes out because it uses the *'-ing'* form in *'coming'* and also because it unnecessarily adds the pronoun 'it' to the sentence. Hence **the correct answer is A**.

The Aristotle Multiple-Split Method

Idiom Split - No Idioms underlined

First word Split

A - that

~~B - in~~

C - in

~~D - in~~

E - that

On the GMAT *'confidence'* will almost always be followed by *'that'*. C is not totally incorrect though, because you can have confidence in someone's ability. Most likely the answer will be A or E but let's not eliminate C right now. B and D however go out.

Last word Split

A - (instead) come

~~C - (instead) to come~~

~~E - (instead) coming~~

The sentence says that the economy will do two things - *avoid* the recession and *come* in for a 'soft landing'. Basically 'avoid' has to parallel 'come' and not 'to come' or 'coming'.

Hence A is the correct answer

A - OA
B - Usage
C - Parallelism
D - Usage
E – Parallelism

Difficulty level - Medium

Q51) The One-Minute Method

The use of '*so*' in the first part of the sentence gives you a hint that you should start looking for a '*that*' or '*as to*' somewhere in the sentence.

a) A goes out because it doesn't contain '*that*' or '*as to*'

b) D and E go out because we avoid the '*-ing*' form in '*distinguishing*' and '*making*'

c) Between B and C, C goes out because it contains the ambiguous '*they*' at the end, so **B is the correct answer**. Also the phrase '*the result of this*' in C doesn't make sense.

The Aristotle Multiple-Split Method

Idiom Split

~~A - so.....it~~
B - so....that
C - so.....that
D - so...that
~~E - so.....as to~~

The correct idioms are '*so....that*' and '*so.... as to*'. Hence eliminate A. Also between '*so.... that*' and '*so....as to*', the GMAT prefers 'so....that'. Hence eliminate E as well.

First word Split - All the options start with the same phrase so ignore this split.

Last word Split

B - to make
C - to make
~~D - making~~

'To make' is parallel to *'to distinguish'*, hence eliminate D.

Pronoun Split - Both the options use *'it'* correctly so ignore this split.

Verb Split

B - hampers, distinguish, make
C - hampers, distinguish, make

Both the options use the verbs correctly.

Check the remaining options for meaning

The phrase 'as a result' is much clearer than the phrase 'the result of this'.

Hence B is the correct answer.

A - Idiom
B - OA
C - Meaning
D - Parallelism
E - Idiom

Difficulty Level - High

Q52) The One-Minute Method

Doing a split doesn't help on this question so we need to consider each option separately. Even though it is suggested that you don't use your ear to answer SC questions, on questions such as this one you will eventually end up using your ear to eliminate some options.

a) A and B go out because there is a redundancy in stating that 'Paris was *her* home' when we have already said '*Josephine Baker*' earlier in the sentence.

b) E goes out because of the usage of '*being*'

c) Between C and D, the phrase '*before to be an expatriate*' in C sounds awkward, so **D is the correct answer**.

The Aristotle Multiple-Split Method

Idiom Split - No Idioms underlined

First word Split

A - To
B - For
C - Josephine baker
D - Long (before)
E - Long (before)

Doesn't help because none of the options can be conclusively eliminated.

Last word Split

A - expatriate
B - home
C - fashionable
D - home
E - Josephine Baker

Doesn't help because none of the options can be conclusively eliminated.

Pronoun Split

~~A - her, it~~
~~B - it, her~~
C - her
D - it, her
E - it

While the pronouns look correct in each of the options, on closer scrutiny you may notice that the use of 'her' in A and B is redundant. Paris can't be someone else's home to Josephine Baker but '*her*' own.

Verb Split

C - made
D - made
E - was

The usage of the verbs in each of the options is correct.

Check the remaining options for meaning

Tough question since we have been able to eliminate only two options so far. From here on you will have to use subjective parameters such as sound to eliminate options. E goes out because of the usage of 'being'. Between C and D, the phrase 'before to be an expatriate' in C sounds awkward.

Hence D is the correct answer.

A - Redundancy
B - Redundancy
C - Usage
D - OA
E - Usage

Difficulty Level - High

Q53) The One-Minute Method

Do a first-word split. Since the part immediately before the comma has the name of an essay, the part after the comma should be a description of this essay. So we do not require a verb after the comma. Also notice that the essay is described using two adjectives – *a critique* and *a vision* - so these need to be parallel.

a) D and E are out because they start with the verb '*critiquing*'

b) B and C are out because '*critique*' is not parallel to '*envisioning*'. Hence **A is the correct answer**.

The Aristotle Multiple-Split Method

Idiom Split - No Idioms underlined

First word Split

A - a critique
B - a critique
C - a critique
~~D - critiquing~~
~~E - critiquing~~

Since the first word of the underline comes after a comma, check for modification. Before the comma we have the name of a book '*Essay on Heat and Light*', so after the comma must come the description of this book. '*Critiquing*' here is used as a verb, so it would be incorrect to use it after a comma. Hence eliminate D and E.

Last word Split

A - vision (of a)
~~B - envisioning (of a)~~
~~C - envisioning (as well)~~

The usage of '*as well as*' and '*and*' before vision should tell you that there are two things that you need to make parallel. 'A critique' is parallel to 'a vision', and not to 'envisioning'.

Hence A is the correct answer

A - OA
B - Parallelism
C - Parallelism
D - Modification
E - Modification

Difficulty Level – Medium

Q54) <u>The One-Minute Method</u>

A very easy question, the moment you read it you should have realized that it is a parallel structure question. Also remember that it is redundant to use '*should*' and '*recommend*' together in a sentence.

a) A, B, and C are out because of the usage of '*should*'

b) Between D and E, E gets the parallel construction right; hence **E is the correct answer.**

<u>The Aristotle Multiple-Split Method</u>

Idiom Split - No Idiom

First word Split

~~A - should~~
~~B - should~~
~~C - should~~
D - eliminate
E - eliminate

The usage of '*should*' with verbs such as '*recommend*' and '*suggest*' is redundant. Hence eliminate A, B, and C.

Last word Split

D - used
E - hospitals

Doesn't help since neither of the options can be conclusively eliminated

Pronoun Split - No pronouns underlined in either of the options

Verb Split

D - eliminate, consolidate, used
E - eliminate, consolidate, use

The verbs in D are not parallel ('eliminate' and 'consolidate' are in the present tense whereas 'used' is in the past tense)

Hence E is the correct answer

A - Redundancy
B - Redundancy
C - Redundancy
D - Parallelism
E – OA

Difficulty Level - Low

Q55) The One-Minute Method

This question looks difficult at first and doing a first-word split doesn't help. So do a last-word split – *to apply* and *applying*. If you have spotted a parallel structure problem ('to move' has to parallel 'to apply') then great, but even if you haven't noticed this, remember you must avoid '-ing' constructions.

a) D and E go out because of the use of the '-ing' form in 'applying'

b) The use of a semi colon in C is incorrect so eliminate C

c) Between A and B, if you spot the redundancy in A (*to be able* and *enable* is the same thing) then you immediately get the answer as B, but even if you miss this redundancy, B is shorter so go with **B as the correct answer**.

The Aristotle Multiple-Split Method

Idiom Split - No Idiom

First word Split

A - programs that

B - programs that

~~C - programs; that~~

D - programs, which

E - programs, which

Both the pronouns *'that'* and *'which'* are used correctly in this sentence. However the usage of a semicolon in C is incorrect since the relative pronoun *'that'* needs to modify the *'programs'*. Hence eliminate C.

Last word Split

A - to apply

B - to apply

~~D - applying~~

~~E - applying~~

Try to understand the meaning of the sentence. It says that the rent-to-buy programs will enable people to do two things - *to move* and *to apply* - so these two need to be parallel. Hence eliminate D and E.

Pronoun Split

A - that

B - that

Both the pronouns use 'that' correctly.

Verb Split

A - enable, move, apply

B - enable, move, apply

Both the options use the verbs correctly

Check the remaining options for Meaning

On going through both the options you should be able to spot the redundancy in using *'enable'* and *'to be able'* in the same sentence.

Hence B is the correct answer

A - Redundancy
B - OA
C - Punctuation (Semicolon)
D - Parallelism
E - Parallelism

Difficulty Level - High

Q56) <u>The One-Minute Method</u>

a) The first word split actually takes us straight to the answer. Since *'of'* is being used before *'both'*, it does not need to be repeated before the name of the second book. Hence eliminate A, C, and D.

b) Between B and E, the use of *also* along with *and* in B is redundant; **hence E is the correct answer**.

The Aristotle Multiple-Split Method

Idiom Split - No idioms underlined

First word Split

~~A – also of~~
~~B – also~~
~~C – of~~
~~D – of~~
E – Women's Work

Since *'of'* is being used before *'both'*, it does not need to be repeated before the name of the second book. Hence eliminate A, C, and D. Also the use of *also* along with *and* in B is redundant.

Hence E is the correct answer

A - Parallelism
B - Redundancy
C - Parallelism
D - Parallelism
E – OA

Difficulty Level - Medium

Q57) The One-Minute Method

Whenever you see *'either'* in a sentence check to see whether its placement is correct in all the options. Here the sentence is implying that the images were fashioned from either of the two things, so *'either'* needs to come after *'fashioned'* and not before it.

a) C and D are out because they put *either* before *fashioned*

b) In A and B, whatever comes after the comma should be modifying what comes immediately before the comma – the Kushan empire. So both these options go out because they make it appear as though the empire itself was fashioned from something. Hence **E is the correct answer**.

The Aristotle Multiple-Split Method

Idiom Split

A – either from.......or
B – from either......or
~~C – either fashioned from....or~~
~~D – either fashioned from.....or~~
E – either from.....or

All the options correctly use *'either.....or'*. However, whenever you see the word *'either'* in a sentence, immediately check whether the placement of *'either'* is appropriate. In this sentence we are saying that the images were fashioned from either of the two things - *spotted sandstone* or *grey schist*. Hence 'either' should come after 'fashioned' and not before it. If 'either' were to come before 'fashioned' then we would need another 'fashioned from' after *'or'* as well. Hence eliminate C and D.

First word Split

~~A - Empire, fashioned~~
~~B - Empire, fashioned~~
E - Empire and
The modifying phrase starting with *'fashioned'* should be placed next to Hindu deities and not next to Kushan Empire. So eliminate A and B.

Hence E is the correct answer

A - Modification
B - Modification
C - Meaning
D - Meaning
E – OA

Difficulty Level - Medium

Q58) The One-Minute Method

A tough sentence, the only way to get it right (especially in one minute) is to go with the option that sounds the best. Since D sounds the best of the lot, D **is the correct answer**. Sorry but we really can't really provide a better reasoning for this; sometimes you just have to trust the ear. Even the OG gives the same explanation, but in a lot more words.

The Aristotle Multiple-Split Method

Idiom Split - No Idioms underlined

First word Split

~~A - That~~
~~B - That~~
C - It
D - It
~~E - The fact~~

Ideally one should avoid starting a sentence with 'that', even though this is not incorrect. So keep out A and B for now. If nothing looks good from the remaining three options then we'll come back and look at these two options. Again the usage of the word 'the fact' to begin a sentence doesn't make sense. It's much better to start a sentence with 'it'. So eliminate E as well.

Last word Split

C – technology
D – technology

Neither of the options can be conclusively eliminated.

Pronoun Split
C - It, it, who
D - It, that

The use of '*who*' in C is not required and unnecessarily makes the sentence longer.

Hence D is the correct answer

A - Usage
B - Usage
C - Meaning
D - OA
E – Usage

Difficulty Level - High

Q59) The One-Minute Method

A very simple modification question, the first line of the sentence should immediately tell you that whatever follows the comma should be what this line is referring to i.e. *some human being.*

a) A, B, and C are out because in each of these, the modifying phrase is referring to Adam Smith's *books* and not to Adam Smith himself

b) Between D and E, the use of '*similar to*' in D is unidiomatic, so **the correct answer is E.**

The Aristotle Multiple-Split Method

Idiom Split

A - books are to........what Marx's Das Kapital is to
~~B - books are to........like Marx's Das Kapital is to~~
~~C - books are to........just as Marx's Das Kapital is to~~
~~D - books are to........similar to Marx's Das Kapital is to~~
E - books are to........what Marx's Das Kapital is to

The correct idiom is '*A is to B ......what X is to Y*'. Only A and E get the idiom right.

First word Split

A - Adam Smith's books
E - Adam Smith

The phrase before the underline is a modifying phrase talking about a leading figure. The figure has to be Adam Smith and not his books.

Hence E is the correct answer

A - Modification
B - Idiom
C - Idiom
D - Idiom
E - OA

Difficulty Level – Low

Q60) The One-Minute Method

A split doesn't help much so let's consider each option individually.

a) A looks good so hold it.

b) In B it is not clear who is '*proclaiming*'. A definitely looks better than this so eliminate B

c) Eliminate C because of the ambiguous '*they*'

d) D looks good so hold it

e) E appears too wordy and awkward, A and D look better so eliminate E.

f) Between A and D, remember that the GMAT does not like the use of '*in that*', so eliminate A and go with D.

The Aristotle Multiple-Split Method

Idiom Split - No Idioms underlined

First word Split

A - world in that
~~B - world, proclaiming~~
~~C - world when~~
D - world, for
E - world by

The usage of *proclaiming* in B doesn't make sense because it is not clear who is proclaiming. Similarly 'when' is not referring to a specific time period in B.

Last word Split

~~A - festival's month~~
D - month of the festival
E - month of the festival

On the GMAT, it's best to avoid the use of possessives as much as possible. Hence eliminate A.

Pronoun Split - No pronouns underlined in any of the remaining options

Verb Split

D - was proclaimed
E - proclamation was

D sounds much more specific and clear than E.

Hence D is the correct answer

A - Usage
B - Meaning
C - Meaning
D - OA
E – Usage

Difficulty Level – High

Q61) The One-Minute Method

The moment you spot *'all'* or *'each'* in a sentence, check for a subject verb agreement problem. In this sentence it's even better if we do a split using the last word – *determine* and *determines*. Since the subject is two things (predominating industries and regulatory environment), the verb must be the plural *determine*.

a) A, C, and D are out because of the singular verb 'determines'

b) Between B and E, eliminate B because the pronoun 'their' incorrectly refers to 'each' state. Hence **E is the correct answer**.

The Aristotle Multiple-Split Method

Idiom Split - No Idioms underlined

First word Split

A - all
~~B - each~~
C - all
D - each
E - all

Whenever you see *'all'* and *'each'*, immediately check for subject-verb agreement. In B 'each' does not agree with 'their'. Hence eliminate B.

Last word Split

~~A - determines~~
~~C - determines~~
~~D - determines~~
E - determine

Since the subject is two things (predominating industries and regulatory environment), the verb needs to be the plural 'determine'.

Hence E is the correct answer

A - Sub-Verb Agreement
B - Pronoun Agreement
C - Sub-Verb Agreement
D - Sub-Verb Agreement
E - OA

Difficulty Level - Low

Q62) The One-Minute Method

Whenever you see a sentence start with an '-ing' word, nine times out of ten you are looking at a modification question. Whatever is rivalling the pyramids should come immediately after the comma (obviously this has to be a monument or an artefact of some type). The only option which does this is A, which puts the *army of terra-cotta warriors* after the comma. Hence **A is the correct answer**.

The Aristotle Multiple-Split Method

Idiom Split - No Idioms underlined

First word Split

A - the army of terracotta warriors
~~B - Qin Shi Huang~~
~~C - it (took)~~
~~D - more (than)~~
~~E - more (than)~~

Since the sentence starts with an '*ing*' word, immediately check for a modification error. What comes after the comma has to be another object that is 'rivalling' the pyramids of Egypt i.e. the army of terracotta warriors.

Hence A is the correct answer

A - OA
B - Modification
C - Modification
D - Modification
E - Modification

Difficulty Level – Low

Q63) The One-Minute Method

The correct idiom is *'try to'* and not *'try and'*. Also notice that the newly elected members will try to do two things, which should be parallel.

a) A and B are out because of the use of *'try and'*

b) C is out because 'restrictions' are placed *'on'* something and not 'for' something

c) Between D and E, E gets the parallel structure right ('establish' parallels 'encourage') and hence **E is the correct answer**.

The Aristotle Multiple-Split Method

Idiom Split

~~A - try and, restrictions for~~
~~B - try and, restrictions on~~
~~C - try, restrictions for~~
D - try to, restrictions on
E - try to, restrictions on

The correct idioms are *'try to'* and *'restrictions on'*. Hence eliminate A, B, and C.

First word Split - Already done above.

Last word Split

D - encouraging
E - encourage

The correct parallel construction is 'to grow and to encourage'.

Hence E is the correct answer

A - Idiom
B - Idiom
C - Idiom
D - Parallelism
E - OA

Difficulty Level – Low

Q64) The One-Minute Method

The use of *'not only'* at the beginning of the sentence should tell you to look for a *'but also'* somewhere else in the sentence. Even though there may be options which do away with this entire construction, very rarely will they be correct. This means that the correct answer is most likely A, but in case you have time you can still quickly go through the remaining options more from the point of view of elimination than anything else. You may also have noticed that *'damage'* and *'aggravate'* need to be parallel; this brings you down to A or C and you always avoid the *'-ing'* form so **A is the correct answer.**

The Aristotle Multiple-Split Method

Idiom Split

A - not only.....but also
~~B - .....but also~~
~~C - .....but also~~
~~D - not only.....also~~
E - no idiom

The correct idiom is *'not only.....but also'*, so eliminate B, C, and D.

First word Split

A - not only
E - are doing

E needlessly uses the present progressive tense to make a general statement. We aren't really discussing an ongoing action in this sentence to warrant the use of the progressive tense.

Hence A is the correct answer

A - OA
B - Idiom
C - Idiom
D - Idiom
E - Verb Tense

Difficulty Level – Low

Q65) The One-Minute Method

Since the sentence starts with a modifying phrase, whoever is digging needs to come after the comma.

a) Hence eliminate A and B because it is the *scientists* who are doing the digging and not the *evidence.*

b) D and E get the use of *which* wrong (*which* is not preceded by a comma or a preposition); **hence C is the correct answer.**

The Aristotle Multiple-Split Method

Idiom Split - No idioms underlined

First word Split

~~A – evidence~~
~~B – evidence~~
C – scientists
D - scientists
E – scientists

Since the sentence starts with a modifying phrase, whoever is digging needs to come after the comma. Hence eliminate A and B because it is the *scientists* who are doing the digging and not the *evidence.*

Last word Split

C – than
D – was
E - that

Doesn't help much because none of the options can be conclusively eliminated

Pronoun Split

C – that
~~D – that, which~~
~~E – which, that~~

D and E get the use of *which* wrong (*which* is not preceded by a comma or a preposition)

Hence C is the correct answer

A - Modification
B - Modification
C - OA
D - Pronoun
E - Pronoun

Difficulty Level - Low

Q66) The One-Minute Method

Doing a first-word split gives you a choice between *'act like'* and *'act as'*. The idea is not to show similarity between the rocks and buffer (in which case 'like' would have been correct) but to state that the rocks themselves will act as a buffer. Hence we need to go with *'as'*.

a) B and E are out because of the use of *'act like'*

b) Eliminate A because of the ambiguous *'it'*

c) The use of 'acting' makes no sense in D, so **C is the correct answer**.

The Aristotle Multiple-Split Method

Idiom Split

A - act as
~~B - act like~~
C - act as
D - acting as
~~E - acting like~~

The idiom *act like* means to behave like someone whereas *act as* means to describe the function of something. Obviously *act as* is the correct idiom in this sentence. Hence eliminate B and E.

First word Split

A - act
C - act
~~D - acting~~

The part of the sentence before the underline says that something *'would rise and.....'*. Whatever comes after 'and' has to parallel *'rise'*, hence *'act'* is the correct usage.

Last word Split

~~A - absorbs~~
C - absorbing

Read the part after the underline. The usage of the phrase *'and protecting'* means whatever comes earlier needs to parallel *'protecting'*. So go with *'absorbing'*.

Hence C is the correct answer

A - Parallelism
B - Idiom
C - OA
D - Parallelism
E - Idiom

Difficulty Level - Medium

Q67) The One-Minute Method

An easy question, doing a first word split gives you two choices – *include* and *includes*. Plural subject '*species*' requires plural verb '*include*'.

a) D and E are out because of the usage of '*includes*'

b) Avoid C because of the usage of '*being*'

c) The use of '*growing*' in C is ambiguous whereas '*which*' in A makes it clear that it is referring to the killer whale; hence **A is the correct answer**.

The Aristotle Multiple-Split Method

Idiom Split - No Idioms underlined

First word Split

A - include
B - include
C - include
~~D - includes~~
~~E - includes~~

The presence of both, singular and plural verbs, suggests that we need to look for a subject-verb agreement problem. The plural subject 'species' requires plural verb 'include'.

Last word Split

A - and is
B - and
~~C - and being~~

'Being' is best avoided and the other two options anyway look better than C, so eliminate C.

Pronoun Split

A - which
B - no pronoun

You might be tempted to avoid the pronoun 'which', but on closer scrutiny the usage of 'growing' in B is unclear and awkward whereas 'which' correctly refers to the 'killer whale'.

Hence A is the correct answer

A - OA
B - Meaning
C - Usage
D - SV Agreement
E - SV Agreement

Difficulty Level - Medium

Q68) The One-Minute Method

Since the sentence starts with a modifying phrase, whoever is outlining his strategy needs to come immediately after the comma.

a) Thus eliminate A, B, and C because it is *the chief executive* and not *his plans* that are doing the outlining.

b) Between D and E, E incorrectly suggests that the plans themselves are doing the cutting; **hence D is the correct answer.**

The Aristotle Multiple-Split Method

Idiom Split - No Idioms underlined

First word Split

~~A - executive's plans~~
~~B - executive's plans~~
~~C - executive's plans~~
D - executive
E – executive

Since the sentence starts with a modifying phrase, whoever is outlining his strategy needs to come immediately after the comma. Thus eliminate A, B, and C because it is the *chief executive* and not *his plans* that are doing the outlining.

Last word Split

D – 18 months
E – 18 months

Doesn't help because both the options are the same.

Pronoun Split

D - none
E – that

The use of 'that' in E incorrectly suggests that the plans themselves are doing the cutting.

Hence D is the correct answer

A - Modification
B - Modification
C - Modification
D - OA
E – Pronoun/Meaning

Difficulty Level - Low

Q69) The One-Minute Method

The original sentence contains too many pronouns but so do the five options. The best answer would use these pronouns with the least possible ambiguity. Also since the sentence is talking about a hypothetical situation because of the usage of 'if', the verb needs to be 'would'.

a) A and C are out because of the usage of 'was'

b) D is out because of the incorrect usage of 'that'; also 'would' is preferred to 'could'

c) Between B and E, the '*it*' in E (because of its placement) could refer to either Morocco or Algeria. B removes this ambiguity by the correct placement of '*it*'. Hence **B is the correct answer**.

The Aristotle Multiple-Split Method

Idiom Split - No Idiom

First word Split

A - if

B - without

C - their

D - without

E – never

Doesn't help because none of the options can be conclusively eliminated.

Last word Split

A - insecure

B - secure

~~C - it~~

D - Algeria

~~E - it~~

The usage of 'it' is ambiguous in C and E, since 'it' could refer to both Morocco and Algeria. Hence eliminate C and E.

Pronoun Split

A - they, it

B - it

~~D - that, they, their~~

In D 'that' can't be used to refer back to 'Morocco'. Hence eliminate D.

Verb Split

A - was

B – would

The use of 'if' suggests a conditional statement, so the correct verb should be 'would'.

Hence B is the correct answer

A - Verb tense

B - OA

C - Pronoun

D - Pronoun

E - Pronoun

Difficulty Level - High

Q70) The One-Minute Method

You could do a first-word split and eliminate C because *'having'* makes no sense in the sentence. On closer scrutiny you may notice that the plural subject *'trenches'* requires the plural verb *'yield'*.

a) B and D are out because of 'yields'

b) C is out because of 'having'

c) Between A and E, the use of *'were arising'* in A makes no sense, so **E is the correct answer.**

The Aristotle Multiple-Split Method

Idiom Split - No Idioms underlined

First word Split

A - that

B - that

~~C - having~~

D - cut

E - cut

The usage of *'having'* seems unclear. The other options definitely seem clearer so eliminate C.

Last word Split

A - but

~~B - but also~~

~~D - but also~~

E - but

The usage of 'also' seems unnecessary since there is no 'not only' anywhere in the sentence. So eliminate B and D.

Pronoun Split

A - that, that

E - that

Doesn't help since all the pronouns have been used correctly.

Verb Split

~~A - have yielded, were arising~~
E - have yielded, arose

The phrase '*that were arising*' in A is unnecessarily wordy. 'Arose' is shorter, so go with E.

Hence E is the correct answer

A - Verb tense
B - Usage
C - Usage
D - Usage
E - OA

Difficulty Level - High

Q71) The One-Minute Method

a) Doing a first word split eliminates C, D, and E because the correct idiom is *combination* of X *and* Y (and not *of* Y).

b) Again doing a last word split eliminates A, because the correct idiom is *endured for*; **hence B is the correct answer**.

The Aristotle Multiple-Split Method

Idiom Split

A – combination of X and Y
B – combination of X and Y
~~C – combination of X and of Y~~
~~D - combination of X and of Y~~
~~E – combination of X and of Y~~

The correct idiom is *combination of X and Y* (and not *of* Y). So eliminate C, D, and E.

First word Split

~~A – endure in~~
B – endured for

The correct idiom is *endured for.*

Hence B is the correct answer.

A - Idiom
B - OA
C - Idiom
D - Idiom
E – Idiom

Difficulty Level - Medium

Q72) The One-Minute Method

Doing a first word split gives us two options – *when* and *in which.* Now on the GMAT 'when' is used to refer to a time period so its use is correct here but remember that, given a choice, 'in which' is still preferred to both 'when' and 'where'. So the answer would most likely be A or B.

a) Between A and B, A can be eliminated because of the incorrect usage of the past perfect tense '*had existed*'. So **B is the correct answer.** Note that if B did not look good to us, we would have gone back and checked the options that start with 'when'.

The Aristotle Multiple-Split Method

Idiom Split - No Idioms underlined

First word Split

A - in which
B - in which
~~C - when~~
~~D - when~~
~~E - when~~

While the usage of 'when' is not incorrect in this sentence, given a choice it's always better to go with 'in which' instead of 'when' or 'where'. Hence eliminate C, D, and E.

Last word Split

A - temperate areas
B - temperate areas

Doesn't help since both the options are the same.

Pronoun Split

A - no pronoun
B - what

Both the options look fine so move on to the next split.

Verb Split

A - had existed
B - existed

Since the sentence does not talk about two things happening at *different* time periods in the past, we don't need the past perfect tense 'had'.

Hence B is the correct answer

A - Tense
B - OA
C - Usage
D - Usage
E - Usage

Difficulty Level - Medium

Q 73) The One-Minute Method

The sentence starts with an '*unlike*', which might fool you into thinking that this is a comparison question, but you will soon realize that the underlined part is not testing you on comparison. You need to be careful about how to do a split on this question. For example, doing a first-word split doesn't help us, we actually need to do a second-word split.

a) A and E are out because of the incorrect usage of '*which*' (doesn't refer to the exhibit in A and doesn't come after a comma in E)

b) C is out because of the ambiguous pronoun '*it*'

c) Between B and D, D gets the meaning across in a much clearer manner and hence, **D is the correct answer**.

The Aristotle Multiple-Split Method

Idiom Split - No Idioms underlined

At first glance this seems to be a 'comparison' question because of the use of 'unlike'. However as you read on you realise that the part with the comparison is in fact not underlined (the comparison is between the National Museum of Science and the Virtual Leonardo Project). This is actually more of a parallelism question.

First word Split

~~A - exhibit, which~~
B - exhibit, in turn
C - exhibit, and
D - exhibit and
~~E - exhibit which~~

Eliminate A and E because both these options use '*which*' incorrectly to refer to 'exhibit'.

Last word Split

~~B - activation of~~
C - activate
D - activate

According to the sentence, visitors will do something (touch) that will lead to another thing (activate). These two things need to be parallel, hence eliminate B.

Pronoun Split

C - it
D - no pronoun

The pronoun 'it' in C has no antecedent.

Hence the correct answer is D

A - Usage
B - Parallelism
C - Pronoun
D - OA
E - Usage

Difficulty Level - Medium

Q74) The One-Minute Method

All the options start with a modifying phrase that is referring to the *earth's crust* (and not to the *earth*).

a) So eliminate A and E because they use '*earth*' as the subject of the modifying phrase.

b) Since all the remaining options contain a *neither….nor* construction, check these for parallel construction. B and C break the parallel structure by repeating '*is it*' after *nor*; **hence D is the correct answer.**

The Aristotle Multiple-Split Method

Idiom Split - No Idioms underlined

First word Split

A – Despite
B – Despite
C – Despite
D - Although
E – Although

Doesn't help much since both *despite* and *although* convey similar meanings

Last word Split

A – it is
B – but is
C – but rather
D – but rather
E – but

Doesn't help much because none of the options can be conclusively eliminated

Pronoun Split

~~A – its, it~~
~~B – it, it~~
~~C – it~~
D – it
E – None

A can be eliminated because *its* incorrectly refers to the earth instead of the earth's crust. B and C can also be eliminated because repeating the pronoun '*it*' after *nor* breaks the parallel structure.

Verb Split

D – is
~~E – has~~

In E the subject of the verb is *earth* whereas the subject for the modifying phrase should be the *earth's crust.*

Hence D is the correct answer

A - Modification
B – Parallelism
C - Parallelism
D - OA
E - Modification

Difficulty Level - Low

Q75) The One-Minute Method

The knowledge of idioms makes life easier in this question. The correct idiom is *'means to an end'*.

a) C, D, and E are out because of the incorrect use of the idiom *'means to an end'*

b) The usage of *'economically'* in B distorts the meaning of the sentence; **hence the correct answer is A**.

The Aristotle Multiple-Split Method

Idiom Split

A - means to
B - means to
~~C - means of~~
~~D - means of~~
~~E - means for~~

The idiom *'as a means of'* means *a type of* whereas the idiom *'a means to'* means *a way/method to do something*. So the correct idiom in this sentence is *'means to'*. Eliminate C, D, and E.

First word Split - Doesn't help because both the options start with *'to'*

Last word Split - Doesn't help because both the options end with *'investing'*

Pronoun Split - No pronouns underlined

Verb Split

A - stressing
B - stressing

Doesn't help because both the verbs are the same.

Check the remaining options for Meaning

If you haven't already spotted the error, note that there is actually only one difference between the two options - *economic* and *economically*. 'Economically' means 'conservatively'; this obviously distorts the meaning of the sentence.

Hence A is the correct answer

A - OA
B - Meaning
C - Idiom
D - Idiom
E - Idiom

Difficulty Level - Medium

Q76) The One-Minute Method

We need to do a split using the initial phrase of the sentence – *appear as* and *appear to have.* Since the Neanderthals are not around anymore, we cannot use the present tense '*appear as*' to refer to them.

a) A, C, and D are out because of the incorrect usage of '*appear as*'

b) The usage of '*for facing*' in E is unidiomatic, so **the correct answer is B.**

The Aristotle Multiple-Split Method

Idiom Split - No Idioms underlined

First word Split

~~A - appear as~~
B - appear to have been
~~C - appear as~~
~~D - appear as~~
E - appear to have been

Because the Neanderthals are not around anymore, the verb form can't be the present tense. Hence eliminate A, C, and D.

Last word Split - Doesn't help because both the options end similarly

Pronoun Split

B - their
E - their

The usage of *'their'* to refer back to 'Neanderthals' is correct in both the options.

Verb Split - Already done in the 'first word split'.

Check the remaining options for Meaning

The difference between the two options is *'to face'* and *'for facing'*. You must always avoid the use of *'-ing'* words, so eliminate E. (*'For'* followed by an *'-ing'* word is almost always considered unidiomatic on the GMAT)

Hence B is the correct answer.

A - Tense
B - OA
C - Tense
D - Tense
E – Usage

Difficulty Level – Medium

Q77) The One-Minute Method

Doing a first word split immediately eliminates the present tense '*reduces*' because the agreement was in the past. Hence C and E are out. From here on the question becomes tricky. A and B use the past perfect tense and D uses the present tense. Since the municipalities are still allowed to dump these phosphates into the Great Lakes, the correct tense should be the present tense; so **the correct answer is D**.

The Aristotle Multiple-Split Method

Idiom Split - No Idioms underlined

First word Split

A - reduced
B - reduced
~~C - reduces~~
D - reduced
~~E - reduces~~

Since the agreement took place in the past we need to go with the past tense '*reduced*'. Hence eliminate C and E.

Last word Split

A - dump
B - dumping
D - dump

None of the options can be conclusively eliminated.

Pronoun Split

A - that
B - that
D - that

The usage of 'that' is correct in all the options.

Verb Split

~~A - had been allowed~~

~~B - had been dumping~~

D - are allowed

In case you are confused whether to go with the past perfect tense '*had*' or the present tense '*are*', think about it this way. The sentence already has a simple past tense in 'reduced'. Now to go with the past perfect tense we must imply that the dumping happened before the agreement 'reduced' something. This makes no sense since the dumping continued after the agreement. So we need to go with the present tense verb 'are'.

Hence D is the correct answer

A - Tense
B - Tense
C - Tense
D - OA
E - Tense

Difficulty Level - High

Q78) <u>The One-Minute Method</u>

Doing a first-word split gives us a choice between *whether* and *if*. 'If' is used to make conditional statements whereas 'whether' is used to evaluate alternatives; hence the correct word should be *whether*. You can even do a split using the last words – *are* and *have been*.

a) D and E are out because of the use of '*if*'

b) Options A and B are out because of the ambiguous '*their*'. Also the correct verb form should be 'have been' and not 'are'. Hence **the correct answer is C**. Remember you always try to avoid pronouns in the correct answer, so even if B looks good to you, you must prefer C to B because C avoids the pronoun altogether.

The Aristotle Multiple-Split Method

Idiom Split - No Idioms underlined

First word Split

A - whether

B - whether

C - whether

~~D - if~~

~~E - if~~

Whenever you are evaluation two alternatives, you always need to go with *'whether'*. Hence eliminate D and E. (For more on *'whether and if'*, refer to the SC Grail)

Last word Split

~~A - are~~

~~B - are~~

C - have been

The sentence is suggesting that the animals' horns must be trimmed before the tourists arrive. So we need to go with the present perfect tense *'have been trimmed'*. In case you are still not sure, do a pronoun split.

Pronoun Split

~~A - their~~

~~B - their~~

C - no pronoun

The usage of *'their'* in A and B is ambiguous because 'their' could refer to the 'tourists' as well as to the 'rhinoceroses'.

Hence C is the correct answer

A - Verb/Pronoun

B - Verb/Pronoun

C - OA

D - Usage

E - Usage

Difficulty Level - Medium

Q79) The One-Minute Method

Since we have a list of names of three countries, the first word of the correct option should be only *Japan* and not something *of Japan*. Hence eliminate A and B.

a) Doing a verb split eliminates E because the singular subject *knowledge* requires the singular verb *was*. Hence eliminate E.

b) Between C and D, D sounds awkward because of the use of *as much as*. C uses *both* to convey the answer in a crisper manner; **hence C is the correct answer**.

The Aristotle Multiple-Split Method

Idiom Split No idioms underlined

First word Split

~~A – that of~~
~~B – that of~~
C – Japan
D - Japan
E – Japan

Since we have a list of names of three countries, the first word of the correct option should be only *Japan* and not something *of Japan*. Hence eliminate A and B.

Last word Split

C – and
D – as much as
E – in addition to

'And' is the shortest option that conveys the meaning correctly and should most likely be the correct answer, but let's continue anyway.

Pronoun Split

C – his, his
D – his, his
E – his, his

Doesn't help much because all the options use the pronoun correctly

Verb Split

C – was

D – was

~~E – were~~

The singular subject *knowledge* requires the singular verb *was*. Hence eliminate E.

Check the remaining options for Meaning

Between C and D, D sounds awkward because of the use of *as much as*. C uses *both* to convey the answer in a crisper manner.

Hence C is the correct answer

A - Parallelism

B - Parallelism

C - OA

D - Usage

E – Subject verb agreement

Difficulty Level - Medium

Q80) The One-Minute Method

Do a split using the pronoun '*they*' which is incorrectly referring to the singular '*citrus*'. A, B, C, and D go out because of the incorrect usage of they/them/their; **hence the correct answer is E.**

The Aristotle Multiple-Split Method

Idiom Split - No Idioms underlined

First word Split

A - to

B - if
C - for
D - if
E – to

None of the options can be conclusively eliminated

Last word Split

A - returns
~~B - them~~
C - returns
D - returns
E - fruit

In B, 'them' incorrectly refers to the singular 'citrus', so eliminate B

Pronoun Split

~~A - them, they~~
~~C - them~~
~~D - they~~
E - it

'Citrus' is singular and requires the singular pronoun '*it*' to replace it. The pronouns '*they*' and '*them*' do not agree with 'citrus' and 'fruit'.

Hence E is the correct answer

A - Pronoun Agreement
B - Pronoun Agreement
C - Pronoun Agreement
D - Pronoun Agreement
E - OA

Difficulty Level – Low

Q81) The One-Minute Method

A first-word split doesn't make sense and you could actually get confused with a last-word split because both *'on'* as well as *'of'* are correct in this case. You need to look at each option individually and eliminate.

a) A looks fine at the first read so hold it

b) B is out because of the ambiguous pronoun *'they'*. You don't even need to read beyond 'they'.

c) C is out because of the use of singular *'was'* with fossils

d) E is out because there is no comma or preposition before *'which'*

e) Between A and D, the use of *'it'* is ambiguous in A; hence the **correct answer is** D.

The Aristotle Multiple-Split Method

Idiom Split

A - dated at
B - dated at
C - dated at
D - dated at
E - dated at

All the options use the idiom correctly.

First word Split

A - sloth found
B - sloth, that
C - sloth that
D - sloth, found
~~E - sloth which~~

E uses 'which' incorrectly (no comma or preposition before 'which') so eliminate E.

Last word Split

A - of
B - on
C - of
D - on

None of the options can be conclusively eliminated.

Pronoun Split

~~A - it~~
~~B - they, it~~
C - this
D - no pronoun

'*They*' in B has no antecedent so eliminate B. In A, the subject of the sentence is '*fossils*' so it is not clear what the singular '*it*' refers to. C and D definitely appear clearer. Hence eliminate A as well

Verb Split

C - was dated
D - have been dated

Plural '*fossils*' does not agree with the singular verb '*was*'.

Hence D is the correct answer

A - Pronoun
B - Pronoun
C - SV Agreement
D - OA
E - Usage

Difficulty Level - Medium

Q82) The One-Minute Method

Doing a first-word split gives you two options – *if* and in *attributing*. Now the phrase that starts from 'in attributing' is a modifying phrase so whoever is doing the attributing (the lawyers) should come after this phrase, but it is actually the perpetrators who are coming after this phrase. So the use of 'in attributing' is incorrect. You can also do a split using the idiom *'attributed to'* and eliminate D and E for this reason.

a) A, C, and E are out because of the use of *'in attributing'*

b) Between B and D, the correct idiom is *attributed to*; hence **B is the correct answer**.

The Aristotle Multiple-Split Method

Idiom Split

A - attributed to
B - attributed to
C - attributed to
~~D - attributed as~~
~~E - attributing as~~

Since the correct idiom is 'attributed to', eliminate D and E.

First word Split
A - in attributing
B - if criminal behaviour
C - in attributing

The moment you see a phrase starting with an '*-ing*' word, check for modification error. Whoever is doing this 'attributing' should come immediately after the comma. What comes after the comma is 'perpetrators' but it is not the 'perpetrators' but the 'lawyers' who are doing this 'attributing'.

Hence B is the correct answer

A - Modification
B - OA
C - Modification
D - Idiom
E – Idiom

Difficulty Level - High

Q83) <u>The One-Minute Method</u>

Doing a first-word split gives us two options – *much* and *many*. Since the different types of dioxins can be counted, the correct word has to be 'many'.

a) A, B, and C are out because of the incorrect usage of 'much'

b) Between D and E, D is unnecessarily wordy and loses out on parallelism (you require another 'that' before 'North Americans'); hence **the correct answer is E.**

<u>The Aristotle Multiple-Split Method</u>

Idiom Split - No Idioms underlined

First word Split

~~A - much~~
~~B - much~~
~~C - much~~
D - many
E - many

Dioxins are actually countable (example Dioxin X, Y, Z, etc), so we need to go with 'many'. Hence eliminate A, B, and C.

Last word Split

D - come
E - come

The usage of plural '*come*' to agree with plural '*dioxins*' is correct in both the options.

Pronoun Split

D - that
E - to which

While the use of 'that' itself is correct in D, to maintain parallel structure we need another 'that' after 'and' as well (before 'North Americans')

Hence E is the correct answer

A - Usage
B - Usage
C - Usage
D - Parallelism
E - OA

Difficulty Level - High

Q84) The One-Minute Method

Doing a first-word split can be confusing so it's better to do a last word split in this sentence. We definitely need a *'by'* at the end to make the parallel structure correct.

a) A and D are out because they omit 'by' at the end

b) In B and E, the usage of *are* before 'by' makes no sense, hence **the correct answer is C**.

The Aristotle Multiple-Split Method

Idiom Split - No Idiom

First word Split

A - not
B - not
C - caused
D - caused
E - caused

None of the options can be conclusively eliminated

Last word Split

~~A - but~~
~~B - but are by~~
C - but by
~~D - but~~
~~E - but are by~~

The construction in this case is '*X is caused not by P, but by Q*'.

Hence C is the correct answer

A - Usage
B - Usage
C - OA
D - Usage
E - Usage

Difficulty Level – Medium

Q85) The One-Minute Method

The first part of the sentence says that something was a goal of someone. So the second part of the sentence must also say that something is a goal of someone. E is the only option which has a subject '*it*' in it to refer back to '*goal*'. Hence **E is the correct answer**.

The Aristotle Multiple-Split Method

Idiom Split - No Idioms underlined

First word Split

~~A - like~~
B - as
C - just
D - as
E - as

The sentence is comparing two clauses whereas *'like'* can only be used to compare nouns, so eliminate A.

Last word Split

B - generations
~~C - did~~
D - generations
E - generations

The use of 'did' in C doesn't make sense because the generations did not do anything, they just had a goal. Eliminate C.

Pronoun Split

B - that
D - no pronoun
E - it

Even though E looks good, it's difficult to conclusively eliminate the other two options. Let's do a verb split.

Verb Split

~~B - No verb~~
~~D - have~~
E – was

B should be eliminated because it does not have a verb whereas we require a verb to parallel the first part (the non-underlined part) of the sentence. The use of 'have' in D doesn't make sense. Also 'have' needs to parallel 'is' in the first part of the sentence which it doesn't.

Hence E is the correct answer

A - Usage
B - Meaning
C - Parallelism
D - Parallelism
E - OA

Difficulty Level - Medium

Q86) The One-Minute Method

Doing a first-word split gives us two options – 'a phenomenon' and 'which'

a) D and E are out because '*which*' is not referring to drugs

b) C is out because of the '*-ing*' in occurring' which makes the sentence very awkward

c) Between A and B, A is out because *a phenomenon* is explained *by* something and not *because* of something. **Hence B is the correct answer.**

The Aristotle Multiple-Split Method

Idiom Split

~~A - not just because.....but by the fact~~
B - not just by the fact....but also by the fact
C - not just because.....but because
~~D - not just because.....but~~
E - not just because.....but because

The correct idiom is *not just because of x, but because of y*. So A & D go out because 'but' also needs to be followed by 'because'.

First word Split

B - a phenomenon
C - a phenomenon
~~E - which~~
'Which' incorrectly refers to 'prescription drugs', so eliminate E.

Last word Split

B - are writing
C - also written

The sentence says two things - drugs are *becoming* something and doctors are *doing* something. So we need another '*-ing*' word (writing) to parallel '*becoming*'.

Hence B is the correct answer

A - Idiom
B - OA
C - Parallelism
D - Idiom
E - Usage

Difficulty Level – Medium

Q87) The One-Minute Method

Since the sentence starts with a modifying phrase, whichever object's path is being monitored by the scientists should come immediately after the comma. Hence eliminate D and E.

a) Doing a last word split eliminates A, because *brightened* is not parallel to *knocking*.

b) Between B and C, the use of *and* in B (before '*it brightened*') makes no sense; **hence C is the correct answer.**

The Aristotle Multiple-Split Method

Idiom Split - No idiom

First word Split

A – an expanding cloud
B – an expanding cloud
C – an expanding cloud
~~D – a large storm~~
~~E – a large storm~~

Since the sentence starts with a modifying phrase, whichever object's path is being monitored by the scientists should come immediately after the comma. Hence eliminate D and E.

Last word Split

~~A – knocking~~
B – knocked

C – knocking

Eliminate A, because *brightened* is not parallel with *knocking*.

Pronoun Split

~~B – what, that, it~~
C – that

The use of 'what' in B is wordy and awkward. Such constructions are almost never correct on the GMAT

Hence C is the correct answer.

A - Parallelism
B - Pronoun
C - OA
D - Modification
E - Modification

Difficulty Level - Medium

Q88) <u>The One-Minute Method</u>

Doing a split using the first part of the sentence gives us two options – those with the verb 'is' and those without it. We obviously need the verb because there is no other verb anywhere in the sentence.

a) D and E are out because they are missing the verb

b) Doing a last word split amongst A, B, and C eliminates A because 'from' doesn't make sense in the sentence.

c) The usage of 'and' in C doesn't make sense; hence **B is the correct answer**.

The Aristotle Multiple-Split Method

Idiom Split - No Idioms underlined

First word Split

A - ozone is
B - ozone is
C - ozone is
~~D - ozone, formed~~
~~E - ozone, formed~~

To figure out whether you need to go with the verb 'is' or not, check for verbs in options D and E. As you must have noticed, there is no verb in these two options. So you need to go with the 'is'. Eliminate D and E.

Last word Split

~~A - from~~
B - when
C - when

The sentence states that ozone is formed *when/from* X reacts with Y. The use of '*from*' obviously makes no sense, so eliminate A.

Pronoun Split - Both the options use the relative pronoun 'when' correctly.

Verb Split - Both the options use the verb 'is' correctly.

Check the remaining options for Meaning

Between B and C, the '*and*' in C immediately stands out because it incorrectly suggests that ozone is formed in two different ways.

Hence B is the correct answer

A - Meaning
B - OA
C - Meaning
D - Verb
E - Verb

Difficulty Level - Medium

Q89) The One-Minute Method

Doing a first-word split gives us two options – *flourished* and *flourishing*. We must always try to avoid the *'-ing'* construction.

a) D and E are out because of the use of *'-ing'* in 'flourishing'

b) C is out because the usage of 'those' doesn't make sense

c) Between A and B, the use of the past perfect tense (had flourished) is incorrect since there is no simple past tense in the sentence. **Hence the correct answer is A.**

The Aristotle Multiple-Split Method

Idiom Split - No Idioms underlined

First word Split

A - that flourished
~~B - that had flourished~~
C - that flourished
~~D - flourishing~~
~~E - flourishing~~

We must always avoid *'-ing'* constructions, so keep out D and E for the time being. Also the past perfect tense *'had flourished'* is not required since the sentence does not speak about two different time periods in the past. So eliminate B as well.

Last word Split

A - civilizations
C – had

The sentence basically speaks about two different civilizations that flourished at the same time. The usage of 'had' is again incorrect.

Hence A is the correct answer

A - OA
B - Tense
C - Tense
D - Usage
E - Usage

Difficulty Level – Medium

Q90) The One-Minute Method

Doing a first-word split gives us *'with'* and *'which'*. 'Which' is correctly referring to 'profits' and is actually preferred because the usage of 'with' is making the sentence very vague/unclear.

a) D and E are out because of the usage of 'with'

b) A and B are out because the singular 'it' cannot refer to the plural *profits*. Hence **the correct answer is C.**

The Aristotle Multiple-Split Method

Idiom Split - No Idiom

First word Split

A - which
B - which
C - which
~~D - with~~
~~E - with~~

'Which' is correctly referring to 'profits', whereas the usage of 'with' is unclear. Hence keep out D and E.

Last word Split

A - fell
B - had fallen
~~C - falling~~

We always try to keep the *'-ing'* constructions out, so let's keep out C for the time being.

Pronoun Split

A - which, it
B - which, it

As discussed earlier, the usage of 'which' is correct but how can the singular *'it'* refer to plural *'profits'*. It obviously cannot which means that both these options are incorrect. **Now go back and check the option C that we had eliminated** because of the *'-ing'*. It does not have a pronoun and, on reading the sentence as a whole, it actually makes complete sense by making it clear which event took place first

Hence C is the correct answer

A - Pronoun
B - Pronoun
C - OA
D - Meaning
E – Meaning

Difficulty Level - Medium

Note: *As you saw in this question, words ending with '-ing' will not always be incorrect on the GMAT. The correct strategy is to keep out options with '-ing' words initially, but if the other options don't look good then go back and check the options containing '-ing' words, just as we did in this question.*

Q91) The One-Minute Method

The best way to approach this sentence is to do a last-word split. The first part of the sentence says that the wines have been priced to sell, so the second part must say that 'and they do sell', not they 'are selling' or 'have been selling'. Since C is the only option with a '*do*' at the end, **C is the correct answer**.

The Aristotle Multiple-Split Method

Idiom Split - No idiom

First word Split

A - have been
B - are
C - are
D - are
E - had been

None of the options can be conclusively eliminated.

Last word Split

A - are
B - have
C - do
D - have
E - have

None of the options can be conclusively eliminated.

Pronoun Split

A - they
B - they
C - they
D - no pronoun
E - they

It is quite clear that 'they' refers to 'wines' so there is no question of ambiguity. Again none of the options can be eliminated.

Verb Split

A - have, are
B - are, have
C - are, do
D - are, have
E - had been, have

Each option has two verbs which need to be consistent. Also each of the options has a 'sell' implied at the end, but the point is that in some cases this 'sell' needs to be explicitly mentioned. It is not correct to end a sentence with 'have' or 'are'; these verbs need to be followed by a 'sold' or 'selling'. But it is perfectly ok to end a sentence with 'do' since 'sell' is implied at the end.

Hence the correct answer is C

A - Verb tense
B - Verb tense
C - OA
D - Verb tense
E - Verb tense

Difficulty Level - Medium

Q92) The One-Minute Method

Like *'either'*, whenever you see *'both'* in a sentence always check to see whether the two things that 'both' is referring to are in parallel structure. Surprisingly, in this case you notice that 'both' is actually referring to just one thing. Hence 'both' actually needs to be omitted from the sentence. Students are usually very hesitant to remove parts from the original sentence but remember that on difficult questions you might have to do so, just like on some questions you may have to insert extra words to get the meaning clear.

a) A, B, and E are out because of the incorrect usage of 'both'

b) Between C and D, C does not contain a verb; hence **D is the correct answer**.

The Aristotle Multiple-Split Method

Idiom Split - No idiom

First word Split

A - Thelonious Monk
B - Thelonious Monk
C - Jazz pianist and composer
D - Jazz pianist and composer
E - Jazz pianist and composer

Both the alternatives are correct so nothing can be eliminated.

Last word Split

~~A - both rooted~~
~~B - rooted both~~
C - rooted
D - rooted
~~E - rooted both~~

Whenever you see the term *'both'*, immediately check the two things that 'both' is referring to for parallel construction. The part after the underline tells you that 'both' is actually referring to just one thing - *the stride-piano tradition of Willie* (The Lion) *Smith and Duke Ellington.* Don't be confused by the 'and' between Willie Smith 'and' Duke Ellington; our subject is the 'tradition'. Since 'both' can't refer to just one thing, eliminate A, B, and E.

Pronoun Split

C - who
D - that

Doesn't help since neither of the options can be conclusively eliminated.

Verb Split

C - No main verb
D - produced

C is a fragment (because it has no verb) so eliminate it.

D is the correct answer

A - Meaning
B - Meaning
C - Verb
D - OA
E - Meaning

Difficulty Level - High

Q93) <u>The One-Minute Method</u>

Doing a split using the first words gives us 'or' and 'and'. Remember that '*between*' always takes '*and*'.

a) D and E are out because of the usage of '*or*'

b) B is out because of the incorrect usage of the plural pronoun 'them' to refer to the singular noun 'language'

c) Between A and C, C is out because of the incorrect usage of the singular 'it' to refer to the plural *languages*; hence **A is the correct answer**.

The Aristotle Multiple-Split Method

Idiom Split

A - between....and
B - between....and
C - between....and
~~D - between....or~~
~~E - between....or~~

The correct idiom is *'between.....and'*, so eliminate D and E.

First word Split - Already done above

Last word Split

A - found
B - finding
~~C - find~~

In C, the present tense 'find' does not agree with the present perfect tense 'have tried'. Hence eliminate C.

Pronoun Split

A - it
B - them

'Them' incorrectly refers to the singular 'language'.

Hence A is the correct answer.

A - OA
B - Pronoun
C - Tense
D - Idiom
E - Idiom

Difficulty Level – Medium

Q94) The One-Minute Method

You can do a split using the first word and realize that options C, D, and E are starting with very awkward sounding phrases. While these aren't necessarily incorrect, the answer is most likely going to be either A or B. In case you don't like these two options, only then should you look at C, D, or E.

a) Between A and B, in B 'higher' always takes a 'than' and not 'over'; **hence the correct answer is A.**

b) Remember if we found a similar problem in A then we would have gone and checked options C, D, and E

The Aristotle Multiple-Split Method

Idiom Split

A - higher....than
~~B - higher....over~~
C - higher....than
~~D - higher....over~~
E - higher.....than

Any comparative verb such as '*higher*' will always take '*than*'. Hence eliminate B and D.

First word Split

A - Heating-oil prices
C - Expectations
E - It is expected

None of the options can be conclusively eliminated.

Last word Split

A - they were
C - they did
E - they did

None of the options can be conclusively eliminated.

Pronoun Split

A - they
C - they
~~E - It, they~~

The usage of 'it' in E is not required. The other two options definitely appear better, so eliminate E

Verb Split

A - are expected, are paying, were
C - are, are paying, did

Neither of the options can be conclusively eliminated.

Check the remaining options for Meaning

C compares 'this year' with 'last year's' (and not with last year), which is incorrect. Also '*expectations are for*' is a very awkward construction.

Hence A is the correct answer

A - OA
B - Idiom
C - Comparison
D - Idiom
E - Pronoun

Difficulty Level - High

Q 95) The One-Minute Method

Doing a first-word split makes life easier. On the GMAT words such as 'distinction' or 'distinguish' will almost always be followed by 'between'. Also remember that 'between' always takes an 'and'.

a) D and E are out because they omit *'between'*

b) A and B are out because they incorrectly use *'with'* with 'between'. Hence **C is the correct answer.**

The Aristotle Multiple-Split Method

Idiom Split

~~A - distinction....between, between....with~~
~~B - distinction....between, between....with~~
C - distinction....between, between....and
~~D - distinction....from~~
~~E - distinction....of~~

When the word 'distinction' is used to show contrast, it will always take 'between'; also 'between' always takes 'and'.

Hence the correct answer is C

A - Idiom
B - Idiom
C - OA
D - Idiom
E - Idiom

Difficulty Level - Medium

Q 96) The One-Minute Method

A difficult question primarily because no kind of split lets us eliminate any option. The only way to get to the answer is to look at each of the options and go with the best.

a) A looks good so we hold it

b) B sounds awkward and worse than A so eliminate

c) C is out because of the incorrect verb tense '*have been first discovered*'. This needs to be in the past tense.

d) D sounds very awkward and not better than A so eliminate

e) Between A and E, the usage of 'while' in E doesn't make any sense, so **A is the correct answer.**

The Aristotle Multiple-Split Method

Idiom Split - No Idioms underlined

First word Split

A - Even though
B - Although
C - Named for
D - Spear points
E - While

None of the options can be conclusively eliminated.

Last word Split

A - in 1932
B - North America
C - North America
D - North America
E - in 1932

None of the options can be conclusively eliminated.

Pronoun Split

A - their, they, where, they
B - where, their
C - where, they
D - that, where
E - whose, them, they, where, they

None of the options can be conclusively eliminated because all the pronouns appear to have been used correctly.

Verb Split

A - have been found, are named, were discovered
B - discovered, are, have been found
~~C - have been discovered, have been found~~
D - are, first discovered, were found
~~E - are, have, have been found, have been discovered~~

Because the discovery of the Clovis points took place in 1932, the correct tense with *'discovery'* needs to be the past tense. Hence eliminate C and E.

Check the remaining options for Meaning

In B the phrase 'where first discovered' is unclear as it does not tell us what was discovered. Also the usage of 'although' in B to contrast 'New Mexico site' with 'spear points of longitudinal grooves' doesn't make sense. The contrast should be between 'New Mexico site' and 'all over North America'. So eliminate B.

Again in C the phrase *'where first discovered'* is unclear as it does not tell us what was discovered. The use of 'even though' and 'but' in the same sentence is redundant. So eliminate D as well.

Hence A is the correct answer.

A - OA
B - Meaning
C - Tense
D - Meaning
E - Tense

Difficulty Level - High

Q 97) The One-Minute Method

a) Since the underlined part is a restating of the belief, it also needs to start with *'that'*. Hence eliminate A, D, and E.

b) Between B and C, the use of *'so…that'* in C suggests that the ancestors suffered an event *in order to* reduce their numbers. This obviously makes no sense; **hence B is the correct answer**.

The Aristotle Multiple-Split Method

Idiom Split - No Idioms underlined

First word Split

~~A – at~~
B – that
C – that
~~D – some time~~
~~E – some time~~

Since the underlined part is a restating of the belief, it also needs to start with 'that'. Hence eliminate A, D, and E.

Last word Split

B – numbers
C – greatly reduced

Doesn't help much because neither of the options can be conclusively eliminated

Pronoun Split

B – that, their
C – that, their

Doesn't help much because neither of the options can be conclusively eliminated

Verb Split

The main verb *believe* is in the non underlined part.

Check the remaining options for Meaning

Between B and C, the use of *'so...that'* in C suggests that the ancestors suffered an event in order to reduce their numbers. This obviously makes no sense.

Hence B is the correct answer

A - Parallelism
B - OA
C - Meaning
D - Parallelism
E - Parallelism

Difficulty Level - High

Q 98) The One-Minute Method

The sentence structure makes it clear that this is a comparison question. Franz Xaver's works need to be compared with the *works* of any other dramatist.

a) A, B, and C are out because they compare Franz Xaver's works with any other *dramatist*

b) E is out because 'more' requires a 'than' and not an 'as'. Hence **D is the correct answer**.

The Aristotle Multiple-Split Method

Idiom Split

A - more than
B - more than
C - more than
D - more than
~~E - more as~~

The correct idiom is *'more....than'*. Hence eliminate E.

The usage of 'more.....than' should immediately tell you to look for a comparison error. Let's see what each of the remaining options compares:

~~A - 'works' with 'any German dramatist'~~
~~B - 'works' with 'any other German dramatist'~~
~~C - 'works' with 'any German dramatist'~~
D - 'works' with 'those (works) of any German dramatist'

Hence D is the correct answer

A - Comparison
B - Comparison
C - Comparison
D - OA
E - Idiom

Difficulty Level - Medium

Q 99) <u>The One-Minute Method</u>

Doing a split in this question doesn't help much so we need to look at each option and eliminate.

a) Eliminate A because of the usage of 'being'. If nothing else looks good we will come back and look at this option

b) Eliminate B because the usage of 'they' at the end of the sentence is ambiguous

c) The usage of two connectors – although and yet – in the same sentence is incorrect, so eliminate C

d) The usage of 'as' to compare two nouns is incorrect so eliminate D

e) E is out because the second sentence of E makes no sense.

This is interesting. We have eliminated all the options as nothing looks good. Now we need to go back and look at the options that are not completely incorrect i.e. A and B. The usage of 'being' is avoidable but not incorrect and even though 'they' is ambiguous in B, it is not incorrect since it may be referring to stars. The other three options are clearly incorrect so let's not bother with these.

Between A and B, the placement of the phrase 'some of them at tremendous speeds' after stars doesn't make much sense. Ideally this phrase should come after it has been stated that the starts are in motion, to modify the rate of that motion. Hence eliminate A and go with **B, the correct answer**.

The Aristotle Multiple-Split Method

Idiom Split - No Idioms underlined

First word Split

A - The stars
B - Like the planets
C - Although
~~D - As~~
E - The stars

Eliminate D because we need 'like' to compare two nouns - planets and stars.

Last word Split

~~A - yet being~~
B - but they are
~~C - yet~~
E - but

Keep out A for now because we need to avoid 'being'. Also eliminate C because it uses two connectors with the same meaning - although and yet - a case of redundancy.

Pronoun Split

B - them, they
E - which

Neither of the options can be conclusively eliminated.

Verb Split

B - are, are
E - are, are

Doesn't help because both the options are the same.

Check the remaining options for Meaning

In E, the repetition of the phrase *'are in motion'* twice doesn't make sense. Also the placement of *'like the planets'* is unclear.

Hence B is the correct answer

A - Usage
B - OA
C - Redundancy
D - Comparison
E - Meaning

Difficulty Level - High

Q 100) The One-Minute Method

Doing a split doesn't help in this question, so we need to read each option and pick the best one.

a) A has too many ambiguous *it's* and is also passive so eliminate it.

b) The sentence *'An executive....makes missing signs'* makes no sense, so eliminate B

c) Eliminate C because of the ambiguous 'it' in the last line

d) D sounds awkward initially but not incorrect. However the moment we reach 'misinterpreting' we eliminate D because 'misinterpreting' is not parallel to 'miss'

e) E is the best option, even though it starts with a 'Being'. It uses minimal pronouns and conveys the meaning of the original sentence in the least ambiguous manner. Also places *'miss'* and *'misinterpret'* in correct parallel structure.

The Aristotle Multiple-Split Method

Idiom Split - No Idioms underlined

First word Split

A - Heavy commitment
B - An executive
C - An executive
~~D - Executives' being~~
~~E - Being heavily~~

Let's keep out the options with *'being'* for the moment.

Last word Split

A - appear
B - appear
C - past

None of the options can be conclusively eliminated.

Pronoun Split

~~A - it, it, them, they~~
~~B - who, one, when, they~~
~~C - who, when, they, it~~

The referent for 'it' is ambiguous in A and C. This leaves B as the answer but B makes no sense ('an executive makes missing signs........?'). So we need to go back to the two options with 'being' i.e. D and E because the answer should be one of these.

Check the remaining options for Meaning

D uses 'misinterpreting' whereas E uses 'misinterpret'. Since this word follows 'or', it should parallel whatever precedes 'or' i.e. 'miss'.

Hence the correct answer is E *(miss or misinterpret)*

A - Pronoun
B - Meaning
C - Pronoun
D - Parallelism
E - OA

Difficulty Level - High

Q 101) The One-Minute Method

Let's start with a first word split. *'Where'* can't be used to refer to 'clans', since 'where' is only used to refer to places. Also *'having'* should ideally be avoided because of the *'-ing'* construction. So the answer should most likely be either A or D; if neither of these two options look good we can go back and check option E.

a) B and C are out because of the incorrect usage of 'where'

b) We keep E out because of the *'-ing'* construction in 'having'

c) Between A and D, D looks better until you realize that *limitations* is a countable quantity, so it can only be modified by *'fewer'* and not by *'less'*. In fact if you notice this error, you can also eliminate E for this same reason.

d) Hence **A is the correct answer.**

The Aristotle Multiple-Split Method

Idiom Split - No Idioms underlined

First word Split

A - whose
~~B - where~~
~~C - where~~
D - with
E - having

'Where' is used to refer to a location; it cannot be used to refer to a clan. Hence eliminate B and C.

Last word Split

A - limited
D - access
E - access

None of the options can be conclusively eliminated

Pronoun Split

A - whose
D - no pronoun
E - no pronoun

None of the options can be conclusively eliminated

Verb Split

A - was
D - no verb
E - having

None of the options can be conclusively eliminated

Check the remaining options for Meaning

This is a tricky one. We can keep out E because it uses the '*-ing*' form in '*having*'. Between A and D, A uses the phrase '*less limited*' whereas D uses the phrase '*less limitations*'. Now 'limitations' can actually be counted (first limitation, second limitation, etc.) and we use '*fewer*' and not 'less' to modify a countable noun.

Hence A is the correct answer.

A - OA
B - Usage
C - Usage
D - Usage
E - Usage

Difficulty Level - High

Q 102) The One-Minute Method

Let's do a first-word split – *wasps, which,* and *living.*

a) C and D are out because of the incorrect usage of '*which*'

b) E is out because the phrase '*it consists of*' sounds awkward; it also breaks the rule of parallel structure.

c) Between A and B, the usage of '*they*' in A doesn't make sense; hence **B is the correct answer**.

The Aristotle Multiple-Split Method

Idiom Split - No Idioms underlined

First word Split

A - wasps
B - wasps
~~C - which~~
~~D - which~~
E - living

The usage of 'which' is ambiguous in C and D so eliminate these.

Last word Split

A - of
B - of
E - all

None of the options can be conclusively eliminated.

Pronoun Split

~~A - where, they~~
B - that
~~E - that, it~~

'*Where*' cannot be used to refer to a society since a 'society' is not a location; also '*they*' cannot refer to singular 'society'. The usage of '*it*' in E is incorrect since it breaks the parallel structure (cooperative, organized, and *it* consists)

Hence B is the correct answer

A - Pronoun
B - OA
C - Usage
D - Usage
E - Parallelism

Difficulty Level - Medium

Q 103) The One-Minute Method

Doing a first-word split makes life a lot easier on this sentence. You obviously require the verb '*is*' because there is no other verb in the sentence.

a) A, B, and C are out because they omit the verb '*is*'

b) Between D and E, '*where*' is used to refer to a *place* and not to a *phenomenon*. **Hence D is the correct answer.**

The Aristotle Multiple-Split Method

Idiom Split - No Idioms underlined

First word Split

~~A - a phenomenon~~
~~B - a phenomenon~~
~~C - a phenomenon~~
D - is a phenomenon
E - is a phenomenon

The phrase *'a phenomenon in which......'* is modifying 'El Nino', so it should be placed next to 'El Nino' and not next to 'Peru'. It is anyway incorrect to have two modifying phrases back-to-back in a sentence. Hence eliminate A, B, and C.

Last word Split

D - accumulated
E - accumulating

'Accumulating' sounds incorrect but move on to the next split if you are still unsure.

Pronoun Split

D - which, that
E – where

The usage of 'where' to refer to a *phenomenon* is incorrect.

Hence D is the correct answer

A - Modification
B - Modification
C - Modification
D - OA
E - Usage

Difficulty Level – Medium

Q104) The One-Minute Method

Doing a split doesn't help so we need to read each option and eliminate.

a) The use of two modifying phrases back to back (*'in her book illustrations'*, *'carefully.....narratives'*) is incorrect on the GMAT. The usage of 'them' also looks unclear, so eliminate A and B.

b) C looks fine, the usage of *which* is correct. So let's hold C.

c) The phrase at the beginning of D is modifying *Beatrix Potter*. This makes no sense, so eliminate D

d) Between C and E, the sentence construction in E doesn't make sense. C definitely looks better. Hence **the correct answer is C**.

The Aristotle Multiple-Split Method

Idiom Split - No Idioms underlined

First word Split

A - Beatrix Potter
B - In
C - In
D - Carefully
E - Beatrix Potter

None of the options can be conclusively eliminated

Last word Split

A - narratives
B - Beatrix Potter
C - Beatrix Potter
D - illustrations
E - and

None of the options can be conclusively eliminated

Pronoun Split

~~A - her, them, her~~

~~B - her, them, her~~

C - her, which, she, her

D - her, her

~~E - her, them, her~~

The usage of 'them' in A, B, and E to refer back to '*illustrations*' makes no sense. Ideally we should use a relative pronoun such as '*that*' or '*which*' to refer back to 'illustrations' – *in her book illustrations* ***that/which*** *she carefully coordinated*. Hence eliminate A, B, and E. Also since only C has a relative pronoun (*which*), you should realize that most likely C will be the correct answer.

Verb Split - No verbs underlined

Check the remaining options for Meaning

D starts with a modifying phrase that tells you that something was '*carefully coordinated with her narratives*'. This 'something' obviously has to be '*book illustrations*' but, instead of 'book illustrations', what follows the modifying phrase is '*Beatrix Potter*'. This is obviously incorrect modification.

Hence C is the correct answer.

A - Pronoun

B - Pronoun

C - OA

D - Modification

E - Pronoun

Difficulty level - High

Q105) The One-Minute Method

Doing a first-word split doesn't help but doing a last-word split does – *is* vs. *has become*. If you've understood the meaning of the sentence correctly, you will have realized that the sentence basically says that the radio was thought of *as* something but it *has become* something else. Hence '*has become*' is preferable to '*is*'.

a) A, B, and E are out because of the usage of '*is*' at the end of the sentence

b) Between C and D, if you know your idioms, you would immediately notice that conceive '*as*' is the correct idiom and not conceive '*to be*'. Also the usage of '*which*' is incorrect in D. Hence **C is the correct answer**.

The Aristotle Multiple-Split Method

Idiom Split

A - conception of.....as

B - conceived of.....as

C - conceived of.....as

~~D - conceive of.....for~~

~~E - conceive of.....to be~~

The correct idiom is 'conceive of X as Y'. Hence eliminate D and E.

First word Split

A - Marconi's conception

B - Marconi conceived

C - Marconi conceived

Though A looks poor, let's not eliminate it as yet. Let's try the next split.

Last word Split

~~A - it is~~

~~B - which is~~

C - has become

The usage of '*which*' in B is ambiguous. The phrase '*it (radio) is precisely the opposite*' doesn't make sense. The sentence is actually implying that the radio '*has become*' the opposite.

Hence C is the correct answer

A - Meaning
B - Pronoun
C - OA
D - Idiom
E - Idiom

Difficulty level – Medium

Q106) <u>The One-Minute Method</u>

It's a long sentence and doing a split either way doesn't help much. So we need to look at each option and eliminate.

a) A looks good so let's hold it.

b) B can be eliminated because it uses the *'-ing'* in 'having'. Also the last part of the sentence doesn't make sense.

c) C also looks fine at first glance so let's hold it

d) D doesn't look wrong but just longer because of the phrase *'has the ability'*. C and A are definitely better so eliminate D

e) Again E can be eliminated because of the use of the phrase *'has the ability'*, which doesn't add anything to the sentence

f) Between A and C, on closer scrutiny you notice the placement of the phrase *'called ….emission'*. This phrase refers to the *technique,* so it should come after 'technique' and not after 'pollutants'. Hence **A is the correct answer.** In fact options D and E can be eliminated for this reason as well.

The Aristotle Multiple-Split Method

Idiom Split - No Idioms underlined

First word Split

A - Originally developed
B - Originally developed
C - A technique
D - A technique
E - A technique

None of the options can be conclusively eliminated

Last-word Split

A - it
B - emission
C - it
D - it
E - emission

None of the options can be conclusively eliminated

Pronoun Split

A – which, it
B – it
C – which, it
D – which, it
E - that

All the pronouns appear to have been used correctly

Verb Split - None of the options have an underlined verb. The verb is *'is'* which is after the underline.

Check the remaining options for Meaning

Eliminate B because the use of two modifying phrases back-to-back at the beginning of the sentence is incorrect.

Eliminate C & D because it is not clear whether the 'technique' or the 'air pollutants' refers to *'proton-induced X-ray emission'*

Eliminate E because the phrase *'called proton-induced X-ray emission'* should be close to *'the technique'*.

Hence A is the correct answer.

A - OA
B - Usage
C - Meaning
D - Meaning
E - Meaning

Difficulty level - High

Q107) The One-Minute Method

Since the entire sentence is underlined, a split may not be very useful. In long sentences it's always a good idea to look for *pronoun* or *subject verb agreement* problems.

a) Eliminate A and C because the plural subject *fixed costs* does not agree with the singular verb *makes.*

b) In D 'stemming' incorrectly modifies 'expensive' so eliminate this as well.

c) Between B and E, the passive construction in E makes it sound as though the electricity is purposely made more expensive; **hence B is the correct answer**.

The Aristotle Multiple-Split Method

Idiom Split - No Idioms underlined

First word Split

A – While
B – While
C – Even though
D - It
E – The

Doesn't help much because none of the options can be conclusively eliminated

Last word Split

A – electricity
B – expensive
C – expensive
D - plants
E – plants

Doesn't help much because none of the options can be conclusively eliminated

Pronoun Split

A- it, it, them
B- they
C – it, it, they
D – it, they
E – they

Doesn't help much because none of the options can be conclusively eliminated

Verb Split

~~A – costs, makes~~
B – is, make
~~C – costs, is, makes~~
D – costs, is
E – is, is

Eliminate A and C because the plural subject *fixed costs* does not agree with the singular verb *makes*.

Check the remaining options for Meaning

In D '*stemming*' incorrectly modifies '*expensive*' so eliminate this. Between B and E, the passive construction in E makes it sound as though the electricity is purposely made more expensive.

Hence B is the correct answer.

A – Subject verb agreement
B - OA
C - Subject verb agreement

D - Modification
E - Meaning

Difficulty level - High

Q108) **The One-Minute Method**

Another long sentence for which we need to consider all the options. Remember that the OG has more difficult questions towards the end, which is why you are getting all these questions together. This won't be the case on the actual test.

a) A looks wordy but there's nothing wrong with it so let's hold A.

b) B sounds awkward because it has no main verb, hence eliminate B

c) In C the phrase 'are *the* more likely' doesn't make sense. That '*the*' is not needed, so eliminate C.

d) Eliminate D because of the usage of '*being*'. While this is not incorrect, we already have A that does not contain '*being*' and looks fine.

e) E goes out as soon as you read the first sentence, which compares *permissive parents* with *children* of authoritative parents. Hence **A is the correct answer**.

The Aristotle Multiple-Split Method

Idiom Split - No Idioms underlined

First word Split

A - Authoritative parents
B - Authoritative parents
~~C - Children of authoritative parents~~
D - Children whose parents
~~E - Rather than permissive parents~~

C & E incorrectly compare *children* of authoritative parents with *permissive parents,* so eliminate these.

Last word Split

A - independent
B - independent
~~D - adolescent~~

Singular 'adolescent' in D does not agree with the plural 'they'. Hence eliminate D.

Pronoun Split

A - who
B - who, that

The usage of 'who' in B makes no sense. Also 'that' cannot be used to refer to 'children' (use 'who' instead)

Hence A is the correct answer

A - OA
B - Pronoun
C - Comparison
D - Sub-verb Agreement
E - Comparison

Difficulty Level - High

Q109) The One-Minute Method

The moment you spot an *'either'* in a sentence, look for a parallel structure mismatch. Firstly *'either'* requires an *'or'* and secondly, the two things that are modified by either (*asking* and *thanking*) must also be in parallel form.

a) B and C are out because they do not contain an *'or'*

b) D goes out because *'asking'* is not parallel to *'thank'*

c) Between A and E, the correct idiom is *'aid in something'*, **hence the correct answer is A.**

The Aristotle Multiple-Split Method

Idiom Split

A - either.....or, aid in healing
~~B - either......and, aid in healing~~
~~C - either......and, aid in healing~~
~~D - either.....or, aid to heal~~
~~E - either.....or, aid to heal~~

The correct idiom is *'either....or'*, so eliminate B and C. Also the correct idiom is *'aid in ...-ing'* so eliminate D and E.

Hence the correct answer is A

A - OA
B - Idiom
C - Idiom
D - Idiom
E - Idiom

Difficulty Level - Medium

Q110) The One-Minute Method

Even though it looks difficult to do a split in this sentence, notice that it starts with a modifying phrase '*Published in Harlem*'. So whatever is published in Harlem (*The Messenger*) needs to come immediately after this phrase.

a) A, B, and D are out because they put a lot of words between '*Published in Harlem*' and '*The Messenger*'.

b) Between C and E, eliminate E because it contains 'being'. So C **is the correct answer.**

The Aristotle Multiple-Split Method

Idiom Split - No Idioms underlined

First word Split

~~A - Published in Harlem~~
~~B - Published in Harlem~~
C - Published in Harlem
D - The Messenger
E - The owner

Note that A, B, and C start with modifying phrases. A and B incorrectly suggest that the owner/two young journalists were published in Harlem, so eliminate these two options. C correctly suggests that the Messenger was published in Harlem so hold C.

Last word Split

C - Chandler Owen
~~D – published in Harlem~~
E – published in Harlem

It appears in D as though the '*labour leader*' was published in Harlem. To make this phrase parallel with '*was owned*' it should say '*was* published'. Hence eliminate D.

Pronoun Split

C - who
E - who

In E it is not clear who does *'who'* refer to whereas C makes it clear that *'who'* refers to Philip Randolph.

Hence C is the correct answer

A - Modification
B - Modification
C - OA
D – Pronoun reference
E – Modification

Difficulty Level - High

Q111) The One-Minute Method

a) C, D, and E can be immediately eliminated because the plural pronoun *they* does not agree with the singular noun *mutual fund*.

b) Between A and B, the use of *and* in B makes no sense because the mutual fund is not doing two different things; **hence A is the correct answer**.

The Aristotle Multiple-Split Method

Idiom Split - No Idioms underlined

First word Split

A – companies
B – companies
C – companies
D - companies
E – companies

Doesn't help because all the options are the same.

Last word Split

A – one percent

B – or more

C – one percent

D - one percent

E – or more

Doesn't help much because none of the options can be conclusively eliminated

Pronoun Split

A – none

~~B – it~~

~~C – they~~

~~D - they~~

~~E – they~~

C, D, and E can be immediately eliminated because the plural pronoun *they* does not agree with the singular noun *mutual fund*. Again in B the use of '*it*' is not clear. The best option is the one that avoids pronouns altogether.

Hence A is the correct answer

A - OA
B - Pronoun
C - Pronoun
D - Pronoun
E - Pronoun

Difficulty Level - Low

Q112) The One-Minute Method

Doing a first word split looks tempting but doesn't help much because both the options could be correct. However, doing a last-word split proves to be of help. Do we need the '*and*' at the end? We obviously do require the '*and*' because the construction began in A.D. 69 '*and*' was completed a decade later.

a) A and D are out because they skip the '*and*' at the end

b) B is out because '*begun*' is the wrong tense

c) Between C and E, E is out because it does not contain a main verb. Also '*was begun*' doesn't make sense. Hence **C is the correct answer**.

The Aristotle Multiple-Split Method

Idiom Split - No Idioms underlined

First word Split

A - which
B - officially
C - which
D - officially
E - officially

None of the options can be conclusively eliminated.

Last word Split

~~A - Vespasian~~
B - and
C - and
~~D - it~~
E - and

The sentence talks about two things - *the construction began* and *was completed.* So we require an 'and' before 'was'. Eliminate A and D.

Pronoun Split

B - no pronoun
C - which
~~E - which~~

In E 'which' incorrectly suggests that the 'Flavian Amphitheater' was begun. 'Begun' is anyway the wrong tense so eliminate E.

Verb Split

B - begun
C - was, began

'Begun' is the wrong tense.

Hence C is the correct answer

A - Meaning
B - Tense
C - OA
D - Meaning
E - Usage

Difficulty Level - High

Q113) The One-Minute Method

Doing a first-word split proves to be of help in this sentence. Remember you start a sentence with '*as*' only if you are trying to show a cause-effect relationship or to show the continuing nature of some activity. For example '*As you are a good student, you will get a good score*' or '*As more and more radios are sold, the profits of the company will increase exponentially*'.

a) A, C, and E are out because of the usage of 'as'. 'As' is not showing a cause and effect relation or the ongoing nature of an activity. It is just stating a simple fact

b) Between B and D, D conveys the meaning in a much clearer manner. Hence **D should be the correct answer.**

The Aristotle Multiple-Split Method

Idiom Split - No Idioms underlined

First word Split

~~A - As a baby~~
B - A baby
~~C - As a baby~~
D - A baby
~~E - As a baby~~

'*As*' is used either to show a cause-effect relationship or to show the continuing nature of some activity. Since neither is the case in this sentence, eliminate A, C, and E.

Last word Split

B - adult
D – blind

In B it appears as though the '*sense of vision*' will be legally blind as an adult. This makes no sense.

Hence D is the correct answer

A - Usage
B - Meaning
C - Usage
D - OA
E – Usage

Difficulty Level – High

Q114) The One-Minute Method

This is a difficult question because it is not possible to split up the options in any manner. The best approach in this case is to read every option and eliminate.

a) A can be eliminated because the plural *starfish* does not agree with the singular *it* ('it' quickly replaces....)

b) B looks good so hold it.

c) C also looks ok so hold it

d) D can be eliminated because the plural pronoun '*they*' implies that the starfish (and not the arm) are replaced.

e) E also looks ok.

f) Now re-reading B, C, and E, C can be eliminated because the second part of the sentence makes it sound as though the original arm is being replaced *by* overcompensating, which is clearly not the case.

g) Between B and E, E can be eliminated because it breaks the parallel construction by making the active '*they lose*' parallel with the passive '*it is replaced*'; **hence B is the correct answer.**

The Aristotle Multiple-Split Method

Idiom Split - No Idioms underlined

First word Split

A – one arm
B – one arm
C – they lose
D - they lose
E – they lose

Doesn't help much because none of the options can be conclusively eliminated.

Last word Split

A – overcompensating and
B – overcompensating and

C – overcompensating,
D – overcompensating,
E – overcompensating,

Doesn't help much because none of the options can be conclusively eliminated

Pronoun Split

~~A – it, it~~
B – it
C – they, they, it
~~D – they, they~~
E – they, it

A can be eliminated because the plural *starfish* does not agree with the singular *it (it quickly replaces….).* D can be eliminated because the plural pronoun '*they*' implies that the starfish (and not the arm) are replaced.

Verb Split
B – is, is
C – lose, replace
~~E – lose, replaced~~

E can be eliminated because one verb is active and the other is passive

Check the remaining options for Meaning

Between B and C, C can be eliminated because the second part of this option makes it sound as though the original arm is being replaced by overcompensating, which is clearly not the case.

Hence B is the correct answer

A – Pronoun Agreement
B - OA
C - Meaning
D – Pronoun Reference
E - Parallelism

Difficulty Level – High

Q115) The One-Minute Method

In case of long sentences, if a split doesn't prove to be of much help, look for the placement of some modifying phrase (there'll be plenty of these in a long sentence). For example, in the current question doing a split doesn't help much. However you might have noticed the phrase *'under provisions of the new maritime code'*. The placement of this phrase in the options can provide us with a clue as to whether to retain that option or to eliminate it.

a) C, D, and E can go out because it appears as though the phrase 'under provisions of the new maritime code' is referring *to large sea areas.*

b) Between A and B, A is unnecessarily *wordy* and also has the ambiguous pronoun '*they*', Hence **B is the correct answer**.

The Aristotle Multiple-Split Method

Idiom Split - No Idioms underlined

First word Split

A - Because
B - Because
C - Even
D - Because
E - Because

None of the options can be conclusively eliminated.

Last word Split

A - stimulated
B - stimulated
~~C - stimulating~~
D - stimulated
~~E - stimulating~~

The usage of *'already'* implies that the stimulation has already started. Hence go with 'stimulated'.

Pronoun Split

A - that, they

B - that, it

D - this

'They' is ambiguous and can refer to provisions/islets/fisheries, etc. 'This' again is unclear. 'It' on the other hand clearly refers to the subject of B - the new maritime code.

Hence B is the correct answer

A - Pronoun

B - OA

C - Meaning

D - Pronoun

E - Meaning

Difficulty Level - Medium

Q116) The One-Minute Method

It helps to do a split using the second words – *then* vs. *and*. We require 'and' because the members did two things, which must be connected using 'and'. Also the two things – *made payments* and *took turns* – need to be parallel.

a) A is out because it omits the '*and*'.

b) B is out because '*taking*' is not parallel with '*made*'

c) E is out because it makes incorrect things parallel – '*made*' and '*drew*'

d) Between C and D, The last part in D is a separate sentence and cannot be connected to the main sentence using a comma. **Hence C is the correct answer.**

The Aristotle Multiple-Split Method

Idiom Split - No Idioms underlined

First word Split

~~A - subscriptions, then~~
B - subscriptions, and
C - subscriptions and
D - subscriptions and
E - subscriptions and

The sentence talks about two things - members *made* monthly payments and they *took* turns. So we need an '*and*' after 'subscriptions'. Hence eliminate A.

Last word Split

B - drawing
C - drawing
~~D - drew~~
~~E - taking turns~~

In E the phrase '*taking turns on the funds....*' doesn't make sense, so eliminate E. Eliminate D because the usage of the verb 'drew' leads to a run-on sentence.

Pronoun Split - No pronouns underlined in either of the options

Verb Split

B - taking
C - took

The tense needs to match '*made*' in the non-underlined part of the sentence.

Hence C is the correct answer *(made and took)*

A - Meaning
B - Parallelism
C - OA
D - Meaning
E - Meaning

Difficulty Level - High

Q117) The One-Minute Method

The word hypothesis is almost always followed by *'that'* on the GMAT. So the answer is most likely C.

a) D and E are out because *'which'* is not preceded by a comma

b) A and B are out because they omit *'that'*. A also has *'being'* in it. Hence **C is the correct answer**.

The Aristotle Multiple-Split Method

Idiom Split - No Idioms underlined

First word Split

A - of
B - of
C - that
~~D - which~~
~~E - which~~

Words such as hypothesis, claim, etc. will almost always be followed by *'that'* on the GMAT. Hence the correct answer is most likely C, but let's hold on to A and B for the moment and carry on with the remaining splits. D and E can be eliminated because the usage of 'which' is incorrect/ambiguous.

Last word Split

A - today
B - today
C - today

All the options end similarly.

Pronoun Split

A - no pronoun
B - that
C - that

None of the options can be conclusively eliminated

Verb Split

A - being, is
B - are, is
C - are, is

'Being' is awkward and best avoided, so eliminate A.

Check the remaining options for meaning

As discussed earlier, '*hypothesis*' should be followed by '*that*' and there is nothing in B that makes it better than C.

Hence C is the correct answer.

A - Usage
B - Usage
C - OA
D - Usage
E - Usage

Difficulty Level - Medium

Q118) The One-Minute Method

Doing a first-word split gives you a choice of whether to start with a conjunction or not. You obviously need the conjunction, otherwise the sentence becomes a run on sentence.

a) A, B, and E are out because they omit the conjunction

b) Between C and D, '*except in*' is the correct idiomatic expression, so **C is the correct answer.**

The Aristotle Multiple-Split Method

Idiom Split

~~A - excepting for~~

B - except in

C - except in

~~D - excepting for~~

E - exception of

The correct idiom is *'except in'* or *'with the exception of'*. Hence eliminate A and D.

First word Split

~~B - except in~~

C - but

~~E - with~~

E is a run on sentence because we require a conjunction before *'with'*, so eliminate E. Also the sentence is showing contrast by stating that even though Mauritius was a British colony, English was never spoken much on the island. So we require a contrasting conjunction such as *'but'*.

Hence C is the correct answer.

A - Idiom

B - Meaning

C - OA

D - Idiom

E - Meaning

Difficulty Level – High

Q119) The One-Minute Method

A very easy question, doing a first-word split immediately gives you the answer. The moment you see the word 'consider' in the sentence, immediately check whether it's being used idiomatically. Remember, consider does not take anything (no *as*, *to be*, etc.). The only option that gets this right is E, hence **E is the correct answer**.

The Aristotle Multiple-Split Method

Idiom Split

A - consider....... to be
B - consider...... should be
C - consider...... as being
D - consider...... as if
E - consider

In its correct idiomatic form, '*consider*' does not take anything.

Hence E is the correct answer

A - Idiom
B - Idiom
C - Idiom
D - Idiom
E - OA

Difficulty Level - Low

Q120) The One-Minute Method

A split doesn't help much because '*which*' is used correctly in the options. Also notice that '*phenomenon*' needs to be followed by either '*that*' or '*which*'.

a) A and B are out because phenomenon is not followed by 'that' or 'which'

b) Amongst the remaining options, it's very important to get the meaning of the sentence right. Global warming is not caused by *human beings* or by *fossil fuels* but by the '*burning of fossil fuels*'. So in this case, the best answer is C – for once we are actually going with the '*-ing*' option as it gets the meaning across in the most effective manner. Hence **C is the correct answer**.

The Aristotle Multiple-Split Method

Idiom Split - No Idioms underlined

First word Split

A - a phenomenon
B - a phenomenon
C - a phenomenon
D - which
E - which

None of the options can be conclusively eliminated

Last word Split

A - fossil fuels
B - human beings
C - fossil fuels
D - fossil fuels
E - human beings

None of the options can be conclusively eliminated

Pronoun Split

A - No pronoun

~~B - that~~
C - that
~~D - which, who~~
E - which,

In B, the usage of 'that' before the verb 'is' doesn't make sense. 'That' should be used immediately after 'a phenomenon'. Hence eliminate B

Again the usage of *'who'* in D distorts the meaning of the sentence by suggesting that global warming is caused by human beings, whereas the original sentence suggests that global warming is cause by human beings' *doing* something. Hence eliminate D as well.

Verb Split

~~A - agree to be~~
C - agree is
~~E - agree to be~~

The most clear expression is to use the verb 'is' with 'agree'.

Hence C is the correct answer

A - Usage
B - Meaning
C - OA
D - Meaning
E - Usage

Difficulty Level - High

Q121) The One-Minute Method

A simple parallel construction question, B should immediately strike you as the correct answer, especially because of the usage of the preposition 'of'. You can also look at it from the meaning point of view. There are three things that have been caused. Now you cannot cause 'split/splitting apart continents' or 'continents' themselves; what you can cause is the splitting apart *of* continents. Hence **B is the correct answer**.

The Aristotle Multiple-Split Method

Idiom Split - No Idioms underlined

First word Split

A - splitting
B - the splitting
C - split
D - continents
E - continents

The list of items makes it clear that this is a parallelism question. Since each of the non-underlined options has been used in the noun form, the underlined part also needs to be in the noun form and not the verb form. 'Splitting' is a verb but when you add 'the' before it, it becomes a gerund i.e. a noun.

Hence B is the correct answer

A - Parallelism
B - OA
C - Parallelism
D - Parallelism
E - Parallelism

Difficulty Level - Medium

Q122) The One-Minute Method

If you have practiced enough SC questions, you will notice that the placement of the phrase *'from a one-page writing sample'* is going to be crucial to this sentence. A split doesn't help so we need to look at each option separately.

a) A distorts the meaning because it makes it appear as if the firm is claiming from a one page writing sample

b) B is out because it is missing a *'that'*; the firm claims 'that'....

c) C is out because of the use of *'-ing'* in 'assessing'

d) Between D and E, eliminate E because it contains the *'being'* and also because it distorts the meaning of the sentence. Hence **D is the correct answer**.

The Aristotle Multiple-Split Method

Idiom Split

~~A - claims from...........that~~
~~B - claims from~~
~~C - claims the~~
D - claims to
~~E - claims being~~

On the GMAT, *'claims'* will be followed by either a *'that'* or a *'to'*. All other constructions are considered unidiomatic. Hence eliminate B, C, and E. Even though A uses a 'that' later in the sentence it distorts the meaning by suggesting that the firm is claiming from a one-page writing sample.

Hence D is the correct answer

A - Meaning
B - Idiom
C - Idiom
D - OA
E - Idiom

Difficulty Level – High

Q123) The One-Minute Method

The first time you read this sentence, you won't find anything wrong with it, apart from the fact that it starts with 'they'. A better answer would be one that replaces 'they' with 'sales', but remember that if such an option is not available then it is best to go with an option that puts 'they' as close as possible to 'sales'. Doing a split with the first and last words doesn't help us much. So let's quickly go through the remaining options to check whether there's one better than A.

a) Eliminate B because '*they*' is very far from the noun that it refers to. Also it uses the '-*ing*' form in 'growing'.

b) Eliminate C because of the incorrect usage of *'which'*

c) Eliminate D and E because they make no sense, hence **A is the correct answer**.

The Aristotle Multiple-Split Method

Idiom Split - No Idioms underlined

First word Split

A - they
B - after
C - in
D - with
E - a reduced risk

None of the options can be conclusively eliminated

Last word Split

A - heart disease
~~B - growing again~~
C - to grow again
~~D - growing again~~
~~E - growing again~~

The construction *'to grow again'* will always be preferred to '*growing again*'. Remember that we always try to avoid *'-ing'* words. So eliminate B, D, and E for the time being.

Pronoun Split

A - they, that
C - which, them

The usage of *'which'* is ambiguous because it seems as though 'which' is referring to *'red wine'* whereas it should actually refer to *'moderate consumption'*.

Hence A is the correct answer

A - OA
B - Usage
C - Pronoun
D - Usage
E - Usage

Difficulty Level - Medium

Q124) The One-Minute Method

Although this sentence looks complicated at first, you can easily eliminate a lot of the options if you remember that *'more'* and *'less'* are always accompanied by a *'than'*.

a) A, B, and D are out because of the incorrect use of *'compared to'* with *'less'*

b) Between C and E, E creates a run on sentence because it uses a comma to connect two independent clauses. C gets it right by turning the first part into a modifying phrase in which *'she'* is referring to the person who should come immediately after the comma i.e. *Lotte Jacobi*. Hence **C is the correct answer**.

The Aristotle Multiple-Split Method

Idiom Split

~~A - less.....compared to~~
~~B - less....compared to~~
C - less....than
~~D - less....when compared to~~
E - less....than

The correct idiom is *'less...than'*, so eliminate A, B, and D.

First word Split

C - Less successful
E - She had been

Neither of the options can be conclusively eliminated.

Last word Split

C - than she had been in
E - than in

E incorrectly compares *Lotte Jacobi's success* in New York with *Germany* (and not with *her success in Germany*). C gets this right.

Hence C is the correct answer

A - Idiom
B - Idiom
C - OA
D - Idiom
E - Comparison

Difficulty Level – Medium

Q125) The One-Minute Method

A mistake students make in these questions is to try to understand the difference between 'doubling', 'twice', 'double', etc. Remember that each of these could be correct depending on the rest of the sentence, so you need to look at the rest of the sentence to get to the answer. Do a split using the last words and you'll get an option between present and past tenses. We are talking about 1910 so we obviously need to go with the past tense.

a) A and C are out because of the present tense '*has*'

b) D is out because '*there were*' does not refer to the amount of acreage

c) Between B and E, B sounds much crisper than E and it also avoids the '*-ing*' in 'doubling', so **B is the correct answer**.

The Aristotle Multiple-Split Method

Idiom Split - No Idioms underlined

First word Split

A - double
B - twice
C - as much as
D - two times
E - a doubling

'Twice' is the best and most clear usage in this sentence, but a lot of the students seem to get confused with the choices. So let's see if we can arrive at the answer using the remaining splits.

Last word Split

~~A - has~~
B - did
~~C - has~~
~~D - were~~
E - did

Since the time period being spoken about is in the past, eliminate the present '*has*'. Also the acreage 'did' something in 1910, so the usage of 'were' doesn't make sense. Hence eliminate D as well.

Pronoun Split

B - it
E - that, it

The usage of 'that' distorts the meaning of the sentence. Also you must have already noticed that the phrase '*doubling of the apples*' sounds very awkward and confusing.

Hence B is the correct answer *(as we had thought after doing the first-word split itself)*

A - Tense
B - OA
C - Tense
D - Tense
E - Meaning

Difficulty Level – High

Q126) The One-Minute Method

On first reading, A looks very good. Also ideally the sentence should start with a 'that' so most likely the correct answer is either A or B.

a) Avoid C because of the unnecessary usage of the '*-ing*' form in 'creating'

b) Eliminate D because the usage of '*to create*' shows intent, instead of showing the cause and effect nature of the way lie detectors work

c) Eliminate E because '*who*' can only refer to '*people*' and not to '*reactions*'

d) Between A and B, B is out because the plural subject '*reactions*' does not agree with the singular verb '*creates*'. Hence **A is the correct answer**.

The Aristotle Multiple-Split Method

Idiom Split - No Idioms underlined

First word Split

A - that
B - that
~~C - creating~~
~~D - to create~~
~~E - who~~

In C the usage of 'creating' makes it appear as though the '*lying*' is 'creating' something whereas it's actually the '*reactions*' that are creating something. Hence eliminate C. The usage of the infinitive '*to*' in D distorts the meaning of the sentence by suggesting that the reactions are being caused *to do* something whereas the sentence actually implies that the reactions, in turn, lead to something. Hence eliminate D. In E, 'who' cannot refer to back to 'reactions'. Hence eliminate E as well.

Last word Split

A - responses
B - in turn

The placement of 'in turn' at the end of the sentence in B sounds unclear, but let's not eliminate B just yet since we can't conclusively infer that B is incorrect.
Pronoun Split - The usage of 'that' is correct in both the options.

Verb Split

A - create
B - creates

The plural subject '*reactions*' does not agree with the singular verb '*creates*'.

Hence A is the correct answer

A - OA
B - Sub.-Verb Agreement
C - Meaning
D - Meaning
E - Meaning

Difficulty Level - Medium

Q127) The One-Minute Method

A very tricky parallel construction question, if you are not careful you could easily get it wrong by making *'liberating'* parallel with *'persuading'*. However you should remember that 'persuading' will always be followed by the person whom you are persuading; it cannot be followed by 'that'. Hence C and E are out. The idea is to make *'turned'* parallel with *'persuaded'*.

a) Eliminate A because the usage of 'she' before 'persuaded' is redundant

b) Between B and D, avoid B because of the *'-ing'* in 'claiming'. Hence **D is the correct answer.**

The Aristotle Multiple-Split Method

Idiom Split

A - persuaded Charles VII to
~~B - persuaded Charles VII in~~
~~C - persuading that~~
D - persuaded Charles VII to
~~E - persuading that~~

In an idiomatically correct construction, 'persuaded' must be followed by a person or an entity. Hence eliminate C and E. Also you 'persuade X *to* do something' and not *'in'* doing something, so eliminate B as well.

First word Split

A - she persuaded
D - persuaded

The sentence states that Joan of Arc did two things - turned and persuaded. So the usage of 'she' in A is incorrect since it breaks the parallel structure.

Hence D is the correct answer

A - Parallelism
B - Idiom
C - Idiom
D - OA
E - Idiom

Difficulty Level - High

Q128) The One-Minute Method

This sentence sounds fairly complicated at first until you notice that it's testing you on the usage of parallel structure. The sentence tells you that the evidence suggests two things – the elephant is *descended* from and its trunk has *evolved* from. These two things need to be parallel i.e., they need to start with 'that'. The only option that does this is E, hence **E is the correct answer**. A lot of students find it difficult to make sense of the phrase 'is descended from' but it's absolutely correct, unusual but correct.

The Aristotle Multiple-Split Method

Idiom Split - No Idioms underlined

First word Split

A - that suggests
~~B - that has suggested~~
~~C - suggesting~~
D - to suggest
E - to suggest

'Evidence' must be followed by a 'that' or a 'to'; it's unidiomatic to follow 'evidence' with an '-*ing*' word. So eliminate C. Again the correct verb tense should be the simple present tense because the evidence *still* suggests something. Hence eliminate B as well because it incorrectly uses the present perfect tense.

Last word Split

~~A - evolving~~
D - evolved
E - evolved

The usage of 'evolving' doesn't make sense because the trunk has already 'evolved'. Hence eliminate A.

Pronoun Split

D - that, its
E - that, its

Both the options use the pronouns correctly.

Verb Split

D - had descended, evolved
E - is descended, evolved

'Had descended' is the incorrect tense. Since the elephant is still in existence, we need to use the present tense to refer to its evolution.

Hence E is the correct answer

A - Meaning
B - Tense
C - Usage
D - OA
E - Tense

Difficulty Level - High

Q129) The One-Minute Method

A pretty simple question, if you go through the options once quickly you will immediately get the answer.

a) A and B are out because the singular verbs '*has*' and '*is*' do not agree with the plural subject *words*

b) D is out because of the awkward usage of '*-ing*' form in 'having'

c) Between C and E, E makes no sense. Hence **C is the correct answer**.

The Aristotle Multiple-Split Method

Idiom Split - No Idioms underlined

First word Split

A - to which
~~B - added~~
C - to which
~~D - with English~~
~~E - and, in addition~~

Ideally 'French' should be followed by '*to which*' to make it clear that something is being added to French. Also in E we don't need to use 'in addition' if we are already using 'and'. Hence eliminate B, D, and E.

Last word Split

A - Italian words
C - been added

Neither of the options can be conclusively eliminated

Pronoun Split

A - which
C - which

Since 'which' comes after the preposition 'to' in both the sentences, its usage is correct.

Verb Split

A - has been
C - have been

Since the subject is plural '*words*', the verb needs to be the plural '*have*'.

Hence C is the correct answer

A - Sub-Verb Agreement
B - Meaning
C - OA
D - Meaning
E - Meaning

Difficulty Level - Medium

Q130) The One-Minute Method

A split doesn't help much so we'll have to check each option and eliminate.

a) Eliminate A because of the ambiguous 'it'. If we don't find something better, we'll come back and take a look at this option

b) Eliminate B because it is not clear what 33 percent refers to

c) Eliminate E because it is wordy and awkward. C and D look better than this.

d) Between C and D, D is ambiguous in its meaning, as in it does not clarify what energy we are talking about in Germany, whereas C makes it very clear that this is the energy produced in Germany. Hence **C is the correct answer**.

The Aristotle Multiple-Split Method

Idiom Split - No Idioms underlined

First word Split

A - while
~~B - compared~~
C - whereas
D - whereas
E - compared

The options that start with 'compared' (B and E) are obviously implying a 'comparison', so let's check whether they are comparing logically comparable things. B compares energy produced in France with Germany so eliminate B. E, however, could be correctly comparing energy with energy so hold E.

Last word Split

A - 33 percent
C - in Germany
D - in Germany
E - 33 percent

None of the options can be conclusively eliminated.

Pronoun Split

~~A - it~~
C - no pronoun
D - no pronoun
~~E - it~~

The usage of *'it'* in A and E is very vague and ambiguous. C and D, with no pronouns, definitely look clearer so eliminate A and E.

Verb Split

C - accounts
D - comes

Neither of the options can be conclusively eliminated.

Check the remaining options for Meaning

Between C and D, D is ambiguous because it does not clarify what energy we are talking about in Germany, whereas C makes it very clear that this is the energy produced in Germany.

Hence C is the correct answer.

A – Pronoun reference
B - Comparison
C - OA
D - Meaning
E – Pronoun reference

Difficulty Level - High

Q131) The One-Minute Method

Remember a term always 'refers' *to* someone or something, it can't be someone or something. Hence **the correct answer is D**.

The Aristotle Multiple-Split Method

Idiom Split

A - 'term.....is'
B - 'term.....is'
C - 'term....are'
D - 'term.....refers to'
E - 'term......is'

Whenever you use the word 'term' followed by a definition of that term, 'refers to' must always follow 'term'. A 'term' always *'refers to'* something.

Hence D is the correct answer

A - Idiom
B - Idiom
C - Idiom
D - OA
E - Idiom

Difficulty Level - High

Q132) The One-Minute Method

Since the part after the underline starts with they, heirloom tomatoes need to be mentioned as early as possible in the sentence. This narrows down our choice to B or E. Between B and E, the use of 'although' in E makes no sense; **hence the correct answer is B.**

The Aristotle Multiple-Split Method

Idiom Split - No idioms underlined

First word Split

A – Although
B – Although
C – Although
D - Grown
E – Heirloom tomatoes

Doesn't help much because none of the options can be conclusively eliminated

Last word Split

A – year
B – cousins
C – year
D - cousins
E – cousins

Doesn't help much because none of the options can be conclusively eliminated

Pronoun Split

A – their
B – their
C – they
D - none
E – they

Doesn't help much because none of the options can be conclusively eliminated

Verb Split

~~A – no verb~~
B – appear
C – appear
D - appear
E – appear

Eliminate A because the verb is missing.

Check the remaining options for Meaning

Since the part after the underline starts with *they*, heirloom tomatoes need to be mentioned as early as possible in the sentence. This narrows down our choice to B or E. Between B and E, the use of 'although' in E makes no sense.

Hence B is the correct answer

A - Grammatical construction
B - OA
C - Grammatical construction
D - Grammatical construction
E - Grammatical construction

Difficulty Level - High

Q133) The One-Minute Method

A deceptively tricky question because if you do a first word split you'll notice a 'that', and 'requiring' is almost always followed by a 'that' on the GMAT; almost always but NOT always. If you go with C you'll be wrong because the plural verb '*protect*' does not agree with the singular subject '*compliance*'.

a) A can also be eliminated because of the use of 'protect'

b) D can be eliminated because the plural verb '*are*' does not agree with the singular subject '*compliance*'

c) Between B and E, the use of the infinitive 'to require' doesn't make sense because we aren't trying to show intent here. Hence **B is the correct answer**.

The Aristotle Multiple-Split Method

Idiom Split - No Idioms underlined

First word Split

A - requiring
B - requiring
C - that require
~~D - to require~~
~~E - to require~~

The phrase 'compliance with laws *to* require' doesn't make sense because the objective of laws is 'to protect the turtles' and not 'to require something'. Hence eliminate D and E.

Last word Split

~~A - protect~~
B - is protecting
~~C - protect~~

The singular subject 'compliance' does not agree with plural verb 'protect'.

Hence B is the correct answer

A - Sub-verb Agreement
B - OA
C - Sub-verb Agreement
D - Meaning
E - Meaning

Difficulty Level – Medium

Q134) The One-Minute Method

This looks like a simple parallel construction question but be careful not to end up blindly making all the four things parallel. The sentence says that the shift work equations have reduced three things and increased one thing. There needs to be an 'and' before the third item in the first list, so basically the correct option will start with an 'and'.

a) A, B, and D are out because they don't start with an 'and'

b) Between C and E, the phrase 'was lowered' in E breaks the parallel structure; hence **the correct answer is C**.

The Aristotle Multiple-Split Method

Idiom Split - No Idioms underlined

First word Split

~~A - fatigue~~
~~B - fatigue~~
C - and fatigue
~~D - lowered fatigue~~
E - and fatigue

The 'shift-work equations' have reduced three things - *sickness, sleeping, and fatigue*. So we need an '*and*' before 'fatigue', since it is the last item in this list. Hence eliminate A, B, and D.

Last word Split

C - while raising
E - while raising

Neither of the options can be conclusively eliminated

Pronoun Split - No pronouns in the underlined part.

Verb Split

C - raising
E - was, raising

The usage of 'was' in E breaks the parallel structure among the three items.

Hence C is the correct answer

A - Meaning
B - Meaning
C - OA
D - Meaning
E – Tense

Difficulty Level - High

Q135) <u>The One-Minute Method</u>

The sentence starts with a modifying phrase – *Spanning more than 50 years.* Hence whatever was spanning more than 50 years needs to come after this phrase. This can't be Muller but *Muller's career*.

a) A and D are out because they start with *'Muller'*

b) Eliminate C because of the use of *'being'*

c) Between B and E, the usage of *'has begun'* in E makes no sense; hence **the correct answer is B.**

<u>The Aristotle Multiple-Split Method</u>

Idiom Split

A - apprenticeship as
B - apprenticeship as
~~C - apprenticeship of being~~
~~D - apprenticeship of being~~
~~E - apprenticeship of~~

The correct idiom is *'apprenticeship as'*. Hence eliminate C, D, and E.

First word Split

A - Muller
B - Muller's career

The opening line of the sentence (*Spanning......years*) is a modifying phrase that tells you something spanned for more than 50 years. This has to be Muller's career and not Muller.

Hence B is the correct answer

A - Modification
B - OA
C - Idiom
D - Idiom
E - Idiom

Difficulty Level – Low

Q136) The One-Minute Method

It looks awkward to see a sentence starting with '*whereas*' but this is not incorrect. Also notice that this is a comparison question so we must compare logically similar things.

a) B and E are out because they compare *tiny tubes* with *birds*

b) C and D are out because they compare *mammals* with *birds' tubes*

c) **A is the correct answer** because it compares something in mammals to something in birds.

The Aristotle Multiple-Split Method

Idiom Split - No Idioms underlined

First word Split

A - Whereas

B - Whereas

C - Unlike

D - Unlike

E - Unlike

The usage of '*unlike*' tells us that we need to look for comparison in this sentence. Let's see what each of the options is comparing:

A - 'in mammals' with 'in birds'

~~B - 'tiny tubes' with 'birds'~~

~~C - 'mammals' with 'bird's tubes'~~

~~D - 'mammals' with 'tubes'~~

~~E - 'tiny tubes' with 'in birds'~~

A is the only option that gets the comparison right.

Hence A is the correct answer

A - OA

B - Comparison

C - Comparison

D - Comparison

E - Comparison

Difficulty Level - Medium

Q137) The One-Minute Method

Doing a split doesn't help much so we'll need to read each option and eliminate.

a) A is out because it makes it appear as though the composer goes into decline after death

b) B and D are out because of the redundant usage of '*regain*' and '*again*' in the same sentence

c) E is out because the verb tenses are not parallel with 'receives' in the non-underlined part. Hence **C is the correct answer**.

The Aristotle Multiple-Split Method

Idiom Split – No Idioms underlined

First word Split

~~A – often goes~~
B – whose reputation
C – but whose reputation
~~D – who declines~~
~~E – then has declined~~

Eliminate A because it incorrectly suggests that the composer goes into decline after death. Eliminate D & E because a person can't '*decline in reputation*'. A person's reputation can decline but a person cannot decline in his reputation.

Last word Split

B - again
C – status

It is redundant to use again when you already have a '*regain*' in the sentence, so eliminate B.

Hence C is the correct answer

A - Meaning
B - Redundancy
C - OA
D - Meaning
E - Meaning

Difficulty Level - High

Q138) The One-Minute Method

a) The correct idiom is *such…as* and not *such….like*. Hence eliminate A and B

b) Whenever you come across an *either…..or* construction, check for parallel structure. Since *on* is coming before *either* in all the three options, it does not need to be repeated before '*exterminating*'. Hence the correct answer is E.

The Aristotle Multiple-Split Method

Idiom Split

~~A – such…..like~~
~~B – such…..like~~
C – such…..as
D - such…..as
E – such…..as

The correct idiom is *such…as* and not *such….like*. Hence eliminate A and B

First word Split - Already done above.

Last word Split

C – exterminating
~~D – extermination of~~
E - exterminating

Eliminate D because 'vaccinating' is not parallel with 'extermination'.

Pronoun Split - No pronouns underlined

Verb Split

C – have focused
E – have focused

Doesn't help because both the verbs are the same

Check the remaining options for Meaning

Whenever you come across an *either.....or* construction, always check for parallel structure. Since *on* is coming before *either* in both the options, it does not need to be repeated before '*exterminating*'.

Hence E is the correct answer.

A - Idiom
B - Idiom
C - Parallelism
D - Parallelism
E - OA

Difficulty Level - High

Q139) The One-Minute Method

Look at the structure of the sentence carefully. It says that '*in no other*' sighting did the comet do something as '*in its sighting of....*' Hence the correct option will also start with '*in*', so **C is the correct answer.**

The Aristotle Multiple-Split Method

Idiom Split – No Idioms underlined

First word Split

A – did its
B – had its
C – in its
D – its return
E – its return

The sentence compares the prepositional phrase '*in no other sighting*' with another prepositional phrase that should follow 'as'. To maintain parallel structure this phrase must also start with the same preposition '*in*'.

Hence the correct answer is C

A - Parallelism
B - Parallelism
C - OA
D - Parallelism
E - Parallelism

Difficulty Level - High

Q140) The One-Minute Method

You can do a first word split and chose between the singular *'has'* and the plural *'have'*. Also remember that the correct idiom is *'dated at'*

a) Eliminate A and B because the singular *'has'* cannot refer to the plural *'rock samples'*

b) Eliminate C and D because the correct idiom is *'dated at'*; hence **E is the correct answer**.

The Aristotle Multiple-Split Method

Idiom Split

~~A – dated to be~~
B – dated at
~~C – dated to be~~
~~D – dated as~~
E – dated at

The correct idiom is 'dated at', so eliminate A, C, and D.

First word Split

B – has been
E – have been

Since the subject is the plural 'rock samples', the verb needs to be the plural 'have'.

Hence E is the correct answer

A - Idiom
B – Sub-verb Agreement
C - Idiom
D - Idiom
E - OA

Difficulty Level - Low

OG 13 Sentence Correction Answer Grid

Q No.	Answer	Q No.	Answer	Q No.	Answer	Q No.	Answer
1	E	36	C	71	B	106	A
2	C	37	A	72	B	107	B
3	D	38	B	73	D	108	A
4	B	39	A	74	D	109	A
5	E	40	E	75	A	110	C
6	A	41	E	76	B	111	A
7	E	42	D	77	D	112	C
8	E	43	E	78	C	113	D
9	B	44	C	79	C	114	B
10	A	45	B	80	E	115	B
11	E	46	B	81	D	116	C
12	B	47	B	82	B	117	C
13	D	48	C	83	E	118	C
14	E	49	D	84	C	119	E
15	D	50	A	85	E	120	C
16	A	51	B	86	B	121	B
17	A	52	D	87	C	122	D
18	E	53	A	88	B	123	A
19	B	54	E	89	A	124	C
20	B	55	B	90	C	125	B
21	D	56	E	91	C	126	A
22	C	57	E	92	D	127	D
23	D	58	D	93	A	128	E
24	E	59	E	94	A	129	C
25	A	60	D	95	C	130	C
26	B	61	E	96	A	131	D
27	D	62	A	97	B	132	B
28	E	63	E	98	D	133	B
29	E	64	A	99	B	134	C
30	D	65	C	100	E	135	B
31	D	66	C	101	A	136	A
32	B	67	A	102	B	137	C
33	A	68	D	103	D	138	E
34	B	69	B	104	C	139	C
35	E	70	E	105	C	140	E

OG 13 SC Topic-wise Question Break-up

Sl. No.	Topic	Question Nos.
1	Sub-Verb Agreement	3, 6, 7, 14, 16, 61, 67, 70, 79, 81, 83, 107, 126, 129, 133, 140
2	Tense	1, 3, 5, 10, 12, 20, 42, 47, 69, 72, 76, 77, 89, 91, 96, 112, 116, 125, 128, 137,
3	Pronoun	7, 12, 29, 33, 69, 78, 80, 90, 93, 100, 111, 114, 130,
4	Modification	6, 19, 22, 41, 48, 53, 57, 59, 62, 65, 68, 74, 82, 87, 88, 104, 106, 110, 132, 135,
5	Parallelism	2, 4, 8, 13, 15, 18, 26, 27, 34, 37, 38, 41, 46, 51, 53, 54, 55, 56, 57, 63, 71, 74, 75, 79, 80, 84, 97, 102, 108, 109, 116, 121, 127, 128, 134, 137, 138, 139,
6	Comparison	9, 11, 24, 31, 43, 85, 89, 94, 98, 124, 125, 136, 139,
7	Style, Usage & Idioms	4, 5, 8, 9, 10, 14, 15, 21, 30, 32, 33, 34, 35, 36, 39, 44, 45, 46, 47, 49, 51, 63, 64, 65, 66, 70, 73, 74, 75, 76, 78, 82, 83, 84, 86, 95, 101, 102, 105, 109, 112, 117, 118, 119, 124, 131, 138, 140
8	Meaning/Sentence Construction	16, 17, 20, 21, 22, 23, 25, 28, 29, 31, 35, 40, 42, 43, 50, 52, 55, 58, 60, 64, 68, 72, 73, 77, 81, 86, 87, 92, 93, 94, 96, 99, 100, 101, 103, 104, 106, 107, 108, 113, 114, 115, 118, 120, 122, 123, 124, 128, 130, 132,

OG 13 SC Question Break-up by Difficulty Level

Sl. No.	Difficulty Level	Question Nos.
1	**Low Difficulty**	1, 2, 3, 4, 5, 6, 7, 9, 11, 12, 14, 15, 18, 24, 30, 33, 34, 35, 36, 39, 45, 54, 59, 61, 62, 63, 64, 65, 68, 74, 80, 111, 119, 135, 140
2	**Medium Difficulty**	8, 10, 13, 16, 17, 19, 20, 21, 22, 26, 27, 28, 31, 32, 38, 40, 41, 42, 43, 44, 48, 49, 50, 53, 56, 57, 66, 67, 71, 72, 73, 75, 76, 78, 79, 81, 84, 85, 86, 87, 88, 89, 90, 91, 93, 95, 98, 102, 103, 105, 109, 115, 117, 121, 123, 124, 126, 129, 133, 136
3	**High Difficulty**	23, 25, 29, 37, 46, 47, 51, 52, 55, 58, 60, 69, 70, 77, 82, 83, 92, 94, 96, 97, 99, 100, 101, 104, 106, 107, 108, 110, 112, 113, 114, 116, 118, 120, 122, 125, 127, 128, 130, 131, 132, 134, 137, 138, 139

If you found this book useful, do check out the other books in our Grail series.

The SC Grail

Here are some standout features of the SC Grail:

- Covers the entire gamut of concepts tested on Sentence Correction, from the most basic ones to the more advanced ones
- Helps you master sentence correction in a step-by-step manner.
- Provides Targeted Practice drills at the end of each chapter for conceptual clarity
- Does not just give pages of theory but also helps you understand how a concept is tested on actual GMAT questions by referencing the Official Guide for GMAT Review 13th or the 12th edition whenever necessary
- Devotes an entire section to what the GMAT likes and dislikes between two options such as *whether and if, like and as, will and would,* etc.

The CR Grail

Here are some standout features of the CR Grail:

- In depth coverage of all CR Question Types tested on the GMAT
- Dedicated chapter for 'Provide a Logical Conclusion' Questions – a new question type increasingly tested on the GMAT
- Brand new 100 question practice set for Intensive practice
- Jargon free and diagram free language with focus on understanding the meaning of arguments
- Quick Recall chapter at the end that provides a quick revision of all CR concepts discussed in the book

The RC Grail

Here are some standout features of the CR Grail:

- Provides a proven strategy to approach RC Passages on the GMAT.
- Describes the question types tested on the GMAT - How to identify and approach each question type. Also discusses the common traps to look out for in each question type
- Discussed strategies on Time Management, Intelligent Guessing, Effective Reading, etc.
- Contains 60 GMAT-like Practice passages with more than 200 questions along with detailed explanations for each
- Topic, Scope, and Passage Map provided for each passage
- Passages divided into three difficulty levels - Low, Medium, and High

CPSIA information can be obtained at www.ICGtesting.com
Printed in the USA
LVOW03s1328270715

447799LV00021B/380/P